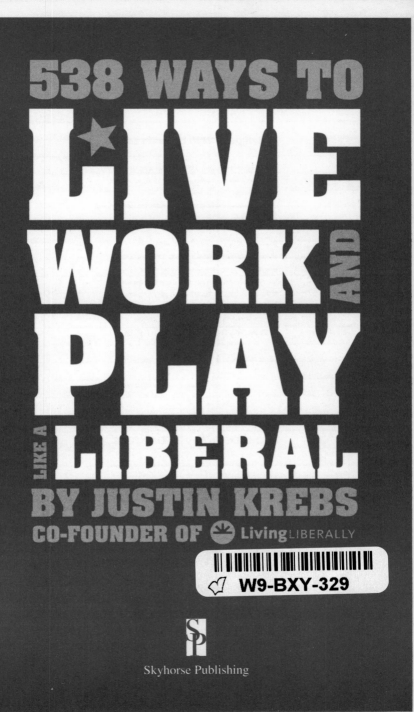

# 538 WAYS TO
# LIVE
# WORK AND
# PLAY
## LIKE A LIBERAL

## BY JUSTIN KREBS
### CO-FOUNDER OF Living LIBERALLY

Skyhorse Publishing

Skyhorse publishing books may be purchased in bulk at special
discounts for sales promotion, corporate gifts, fund-raising, or
educational purposes. Special editions can also be created to
specifications. For details, contact the Special Sales Department,
Skyhorse Publishing, 555 Eighth Avenue, Suite 903, New York, NY
10018 or info@skyhorsepublishing.com

www.skyhorsepublishing.com

10   9   8   7   6   5   4   3   2   1

Library of Congress Cataloging-in-Publication Data

Krebs, Justin.

538 ways to live, work & play
like a liberal / by Justin Krebs.

p. cm.

ISBN 978-1-60239-982-2
(PBK. : ALK. PAPER)

1. Liberalism--United States. I. Title.
II. Title: Five hundred thirty-eight
ways to live, work & play like a liberal.

JC574.2.U6.K75     2010

320.51'30973 — DC22

2010005918

**Printed in Canada**

# INTRODUCTION — 1

# LIVING LIBERALLY — 9

LIVING LIBERALLY IN YOUR EVERY-DAY LIFE — 19

# WORKING LIBERALLY — 47

# PLAYING LIBERALLY — 73

# LEARNING LIBERALLY — 115

# SPENDING LIBERALLY — 161

# ACTING LIBERALLY — 189

# CONCLUSION — 209

# APPENDIX — 215

# INTRO DUCTION

My name is Justin Krebs . . . and I'm a proud American liberal.

If you think you just read the opening words of a support group—well, maybe you have. When you're politically vocal in this country, you sometimes need all the support you can get. Especially when you are willing to use the original "L Word."

Liberal. It's a dirty word that's finding its way back into fashion. Sure, it was once hurled as an insult, but that is so 1988. We're in a new millennium, a new presidency, and there are new cultural and political norms on the rise. It's not so bad to be liberal anymore.

While many once shunned it, more and more of us embrace the liberal label—"Proud Liberal" . . . "Unapologetic Liberal" . . . "Card-carrying Liberal."

What does it actually mean?

Does it mean to be engaged in the humanities in a well-rounded way like the "liberal arts"? Or is it a brand of thoughtless, reckless social programming as Reagan and his conservative cadre would have snarled? In the 1800s, it indicated hands-off economic policies; in the 1950s, it was the national consensus at the center of which President Eisenhower found himself. In Canada, it's the conservative-centrist party. In 2008, it was a label Senators (and leading presidential candidates) Obama and Clinton saw as too leftist for their campaigns.

For all that folks toss the word around, few try to define it. We generally agree that it's to the left on our political spectrum, but do we know what it is beyond that? More than "not being conservative" or—as was popular for eight years—"being different than President George W. Bush," what do liberals believe?

Most people would rather not have to define labels too carefully, whether they are flinging them at others or applying to themselves. But if I'm going to make the claim that this book will relate how you can "live liberally" in your everyday life, I better give a try at a definition.

So here goes.

> **Liberals believe that we are better off when we live for each other than when we live only for ourselves.**

There. That was simple.

Wait! That definition was short and straightforward! It didn't tackle every possible policy consideration, didn't articulate a four-point plan, and isn't rooted in the most tangled political arguments of today!

If that's what you were thinking, you're in for a surprise. "Liberal," as a political approach, isn't strictly tied to current debates. Liberals don't define our political principles by the stances we take on particular issues. Issues come and go . . . one election you're arguing over civil unions, and the next year there's consensus on that and you're arguing over marriage equality. Instead, our stances flow from this principle: We all are in this together.

Being liberal is not only a political philosophy—liberal is how you live your life and interact with neighbors, coworkers, and strangers on the street. It's not just how you vote on Election Day, but how you vote with your wallet every day. It's not only what you chant at a rally, but what you laugh at or rock out to on your iPod.

It all comes down to an approach to life that acknowledges that we're sharing this planet, sharing our cities and roads, sharing our fortunes and even our misfortunes, sharing our resources and our surpluses, our creative impulses and pleasures, even sharing our weather, with those around us. We all truly are in it—in all of it—together.

**We are better off when we live for each other than when we live only for ourselves.** Liberals believe that government is a tool to advance common prosperity. We believe that diversity—in backgrounds and of ideas—is a strength. We believe that creativity and science are necessary assets for creating more wealth and opportunity for all people. We believe that where one comes from shouldn't lock him or her out of the chance to succeed. We believe that we are all in the same boat, and we want everyone else to prosper as well because our fates are interlocked. This means cherishing the environment, cultivating peace, and working with other nations, other communities, and our neighbors to develop solutions that work well for all of us.

And that's just the political side. As a lifestyle, "living liberally" is

★ living collectively—investing in and drawing from common resources

★ living creatively and expressively, because communication and connection build community

★ living sustainably, because we need to green our
society so it will work for all of us and for future
generations—not just 50 years from now, but 500,
even 5,000

★ living diversely, because what unites us is
strengthened by the range of experiences and
cultures we represent

★ living freely and joyously, because life's too short
to be unhappy.

This is not a historical definition of liberal. It's not an etymo-
logical definition. I hope it's not a temporal definition. It's my
belief—and it's the set of values that drives so many good people
and shapes so many strong communities.

It's how I try to live liberally . . . and I hope over the next 538
ideas, tips, and steps, it may become how you, more consciously,
live liberally too.

## What You're Going to Find in This Book

I fully believe that every day, in some of the most routine activities, you can be living out your progressive values. And I believe
that there are some ways you're already doing so and might
not know it.

The purpose of this book is to spark your imagination with
a combination of anecdotes and examples of how others are
living liberally, some simple steps you could consider, and some

ways I'm trying to make my politics personal and my personal politics public.

There is no one way to be "liberal," of course—that's in the very nature of being liberal. And life can be full of contradictions. Is it more important to buy a book by a progressive author to support those ideas, or to not buy it because you want to reduce consumption and could just borrow it from the library? Should we celebrate cars that run on renewable energy, or push to decrease car culture entirely? Is it better to vote for an independent party candidate for the diversity of ideas, or to become the liberal wing of a more powerful party?

I welcome those debates and look forward to well-meaning liberals disagreeing with a healthy portion of this book. These aren't "the ways" to live like a liberal—they are "some ways."

Some are startlingly simple, and that's as it should be. Nobody should expect you to dramatically and suddenly change your life; I'm not sure I have ever suddenly changed my lifestyle. But by doing a few of the easier acts regularly, it may create new habits that will come to feel routine.

Some of the ideas are hard, or even uncomfortable. You don't have to do them all. Just think about them. If you try some of them, ask yourself, "why not try more?" Alternatively, suggest a way you can do something similar that's more comfortable and accessible for you.

The numbered ideas running throughout this book include things to read, watch, and buy; questions to ask; and new ways to relate to friends, coworkers, and neighbors. The magic number "538" is a weighted political number: the total electoral votes we tally each presidential election. However, our politics shapes our lives on more than just Election Day, so these 538 ideas are concepts to play with, organizations to learn about, and choices to consider in your everyday life. There will be anecdotes. There will be how-to sections. There will be lists, sidebars, and the occasional guest contributor. There will not be everything.

There are thousands of businesses and grassroots groups doing incredible work, and I only mention a few; there are thousands of considerations as to what you buy, what you teach your children, where you can go for vacation, and I only have so much room. Amazing innovations take place around the country, but a disproportionate number included here are New York City–centric . . . because it's what I know best. I do look forward to hearing from you about what you know best— because I know there are incredible examples of the liberal life in all fifty states.

So where you see those gaps, do the most liberal thing you can: share your knowledge. Share it with me, share it with other friends, share it with whomever you give the book to next. This would be a dull conversation if I were the only person who had anything to say.

## So Let's Get Started

. . . But before we do, I want to share one other pretty good definition of liberal floating around (but if I'd written it first, you would have ignored mine). It was spoken by a man who had been insulted as a "liberal" and decided not to roll over, but to defend himself:

> *"What do our opponents mean when they apply to us the label 'Liberal?' If by 'Liberal' they mean, as they want people to believe, someone who is soft in his policies abroad, who is against local govern- ment, and who is unconcerned with the taxpayer's*

*dollar, then . . . we are not that kind of 'Liberal.' But*
*if by a 'Liberal' they mean someone who looks ahead*
*and not behind, someone who welcomes new ideas*
*without rigid reactions, someone who cares about*
*the welfare of the people—their health, their housing,*
*their schools, their jobs, their civil rights, and their*
*civil liberties—someone who believes we can break*
*through the stalemate and suspicions that grip us in*
*our policies abroad, if that is what they mean by a*
*'Liberal,' then I'm proud to say I'm a 'Liberal.'"*

That was then-senator John F. Kennedy in September 1960. He
believed in living liberally.

# CHAPTER 1
# LIVING
# LIBERALLY

> *Somebody came along and said "liberal" means "soft on crime, soft on drugs, soft on Communism, soft on defense, and we're gonna tax you back to the Stone Age because people shouldn't have to go to work if they don't want to." And instead of saying, "Well, excuse me, you right-wing, reactionary, xenophobic, homophobic, anti-education, anti-choice, pro-gun, Leave it to Beaver trip back to the '50s," we cowered in the corner and said, "Please don't hurt me."*
>
> —BRUNO GIANELLI, *THE WEST WING*

This impulse to make politics fun was on our minds when my friend Matt O'Neill and I decided to start a weekly political drinking club in 2003. Fun wasn't the end goal; it was the essential means.

We were frustrated New York liberals. We had just seen our country march to the drumbeat of war and invade a country we didn't need to attack. We felt that the authoritarianism and arrogance of the Bush administration needed a response, and yet the public and press seemed speechless. Where were the effective leaders of the left?

We wanted to vent, and we wanted to find a way to make a difference. We believed that there was more that liberals in New York—with a surplus of time and creativity—could do. But we also realized we couldn't change national politics until we started locally.

Many of our own friends weren't even talking politics. We knew they shared our values and our frustration, yet we weren't engaging with them around the issues that pushed all of us. We wondered why. In truth, even in a liberal city, you're not "supposed" to talk politics in social settings. This was driven home one night when a friend and I brought voter registration forms to a bar. We approached a circle of twenty-somethings, one of whom we knew, and asked if they were registered to vote. All of them said yes, except one. When we asked if he'd like to take a minute, he said he didn't believe in voting. When—clearly shocked—we asked why, the woman we knew in the circle spoke up.

"Hey, let's not talk about politics. We're out at a bar . . . we all came here to have fun."

Furthermore, people are busy. Our friends had jobs, and in addition to their workdays, they had relationships and time at the gym and volunteer projects. Asking them to get more involved in political conversation sounded like asking them to make more time in their week . . . which they just didn't have.

Finally, the opportunities to step up into politics were slim. If you have limited time, do you want to start dedicating it to those over-earnest screechers that think politics is all work and no play? We attended a few meetings of groups aimed at younger progressives and found out they typically seemed like a high school Model United Nations club, deeply concerned with following *Robert's Rules of Order* and filled with people eager to become part of the party machinery. I remember one meeting that spent a good amount of time determining whether the agenda was in the proper order.

Politics wasn't fun; people were busy; young political groups were lame . . . so how could Matt and I get our friends a little more politically involved?

We figured we needed to bring politics to the natural habitat of our generation: a bar. We needed to make it part of our friends' social life, not something they suspended their life to join. We needed to make it easy and fun. So we decided to start a weekly gathering in our local dive bar where people knew politics would be on the table.

From the start, there was no hard-driving agenda. We figured that folks who decided to come would probably bring their own agendas . . . and they did. Other people, who had spent their days spitting mad at their computer screens, came and vented and shared and found out they weren't alone.

It also made it an easy place for less political people to come. If you were interested in politics, but felt like you didn't know much, we gave you an easy way in. You're not asked to make a presentation or debate an issue; you very naturally learn more about the topics of the day from other attendees.

And if you didn't want to talk politics, you didn't have to. You might just start showing up because you know it's a group of friends and friends-of-friends who are welcoming, social, chatty. We didn't see those less-political folks as a distraction. We understood from the start that we needed a scene open to all . . . and we just had to believe that even if you didn't come for the politics, just by being there some of the politics would rub off on you.

We decided to meet every week. We wanted the regularity so people would always know when and where it was. They wouldn't have to come to any given Thursday, because they would know it was *every* Thursday. It made it easier to drop in and drop out, and it meant people didn't have to join an e-mail list. They always knew where we'd be.

The frequency created a sense of continuity. It was like an ongoing conversation. People could pick up where they'd left off the week before. Folks would start recognizing each other. We were really building a community.

We chose the perfect bar for it. Rudy's, a classic dive bar in Hell's Kitchen, on the west side of Manhattan, was known for cheap beer by the pitcher and free hot dogs. It had a great backyard that made gatherings of unpredictable size easy to fit in, and management that liked us because we were already regulars. It was a storied place: it was a speakeasy during Prohibition and became one of the first legitimate bars in the city after Prohibition was repealed. It was also known for a colorful, mixed crowd—Hell's Kitchen old-timers sharing the bar with aspiring actors working in the nearby theater district, joined by some folks in transit uniforms getting off long shifts on the subways, and others in suits who represented the neighborhood's newly gentrifying population. These people were used to sharing the crowded bar, sometimes sharing the few booths, and even sharing a pitcher. What better place to stir up inclusive, diverse, political conversation?

Rudy's had had the informal slogan: "Is the person next to you an artist, a poet, or just a drunk? You never know at Rudy's." Now they could add "liberal" to the list.

In May 2003, we began our weekly democratic drinking club. Our friends came, and soon after they brought their friends.

Then we started getting people who'd heard about us—in a newspaper listing, a forwarded e-mail, or on the nascent blogs. As strangers started arriving to become our companions, our meetings really took off.

It was one of those regulars—a guy named Owen Roth who had learned about us from the blogger Atrios—who said: "You guys need a better name for this," rather than "Democrats and Drinks" or "Buttons and Beer," as we sometimes called it.

"OK, come up with one," we said.

"How about 'Drinking Liberally'?" Thank goodness we had no egos and could grab a good idea when we heard it, and thank goodness Owen was willing to share his good idea for the greater good.

And Drinking Liberally was born.

1

Over the next year, the weekly meetings at Rudy's became a destination for liberals looking for new friends, activists with big ideas they wanted to bounce off people who would listen, candidates and their staff seeking to tap into a new pool of political energy, and reporters who wanted to get the liberal reaction to something in the news—at that time, chiefly, the Democratic presidential primary.

Authors wanted to stop by and speak. Filmmakers asked how they could attract our community to their run at a local independent movie theater. Office-seekers asked if they could say a few words. Entrepreneurs came by to peddle politically themed gifts. The growing network of other new progressive groups— born in that same era of frustration, empowered by the internet and energized by the upcoming election—collaborated with us on debate-watch parties, fundraisers, and media events.

A full year later, we were still doing what was at our core: meeting every Thursday night. By then, we were also a planning hub for progressive activities during the Republican National Convention, which was coming to New York. We had become known to blogs around the country, including the growing phenomenon of Daily Kos. By the summer of 2004, what had started as our small group of friends marked its anniversary by overcrowding the backyard of Rudy's. One of the attendees was a *Newsweek* reporter—and a few weeks later, a photograph of a button boasting "I Only Drink With Liberals" appeared in the magazine.

The new and traditional media gave the club a boost, but something more personal changed our organization's course. A friend named Andrew Hoppin moved from New York to San Francisco and asked to start a Drinking Liberally chapter there because he'd miss coming to Rudy's. We said yes, of course, then quickly figured out what "rules" he'd need to follow to be a chapter.

We were also fortunate that a new friend and ally named David Alpert had recently teamed up with us. David created a quick and easy website that showcased a map of the country with dots for the Drinking Liberally chapters: one in New York City and one in San Francisco.

"David," I asked, "should we really make the map so prominent? It does confirm the idea that liberals are only on the coasts."

"It will fill in," David replied confidently.

Our national network was born.

Since then, the map has filled in. We expanded to Oakland, then to our first "red state" chapter in Houston. Then our fifth group launched in September 2004, in Boise, Idaho. That's when we knew we were really onto something. Soon enough we were in all the predictable places for a progressive social club: Philadelphia, Boston, Ithaca. But we were also finding strong clusters in Iowa, defiant liberals in rural Texas, and a dynamic group in Salt Lake City, at the heart of a state not known for liberals or drinking. Another friend we had bonded with through our weekly gatherings, Katrina Baker, joined us as a partner and gave us a link to our liberal siblings across the United States.

Drinking Liberally has expanded to all fifty states and has several international chapters (the deputy prime minister of New Zealand has attended his local gathering). There are more than three hundred happy hours that meet in big cities and small towns. Some meet weekly, some monthly; all keep that feature of regularity. Each is organized by local volunteer hosts who contacted us to start a chapter; those hosts set the vibe, which varies widely from city to city.

When we started we said we were a group for young people looking to socialize around progressive politics. When the Pittsburgh chapter sent us a group photo and we saw six beefy, gray-bearded men at a table, we knew we shouldn't think of ourselves as a young persons' club anymore.

We've become intergenerational. In many of the smaller towns and redder states, the hosts are middle-aged or older, people who have fought liberal battles for decades but often felt alone. Drinking Liberally helps them find their community.

In some cities like Kansas City, chapters even choose family-friendly restaurants so children can hear people talking politics . . . and join the conversation.

Some chapters, like those in Minneapolis and Philadelphia, have guest speakers and regularly invite candidates for Senate and Congress. Others, including New York City, keep it purely social. The flexibility has allowed Drinking Liberally to grow.

As people have brought their own ideas to it, it has expanded with their imprint.

This sense of expansion led us to create other "Liberally" events. Drinking Liberally has never been about the drinking . . . it's about progressive politics in a social setting. Why not other social settings, like comedy clubs? Thus, "Laughing Liberally" was born. Featuring a mix of established and up-and-coming comedians, these shows serve the performers as much as the audience. Comics are often told to stay away from political material in mainstream clubs; we give them the chance to go as far left as they want. Attendees have the opportunity to know they're not going to suffer an evening of homophobic and sexist material and that they can comfortably meet the other liberals sitting around them.

Chapters around the country started hosting book clubs—"Reading Liberally." These gatherings promote progressive voices and often support independent publishers. They have become natural destinations for book tours as well. Authors who have made Reading Liberally a core partner to their tours range from Andy Stern, the head of the labor union SEIU, to top blogger Markos Moulitsas Zuniga of Daily Kos, to Jeffrey Feldman, a smart, insightful blogger/author whose small publisher may not otherwise have had resources to create events around the country.

Other chapters decided that in addition to drinking they wanted to watch films, and "Screening Liberally" came to life. Whether gathering around wide releases or independent documentaries, these clubs offer one more avenue for the non-drinker to find a local liberal community. Moreover, these groups have become a resource for distributors of progressive films by connecting such work with an audience hungry for it. From the widely publicized *Food, Inc.,* to the Oscar-nominated *Trouble the Water,* to the high-profile *Milk,* to the lesser-known but critically acclaimed

*Crawford*, films find a willing partner in Screening Liberally events across the country.

In New York, a couple that loved the idea of Drinking Liberally but didn't like to drink on an empty stomach started "Eating Liberally," which hosts meals, guest speakers, and films around food, policy, and sustainability issues. They also happen to be amazing cooks, and every event features food that reflects our political and gustatory tastes.

As this network grew, our vision of it grew as well, and Matt, Katrina, David, and I formed "Living Liberally," a network of social communities and events, a hub for the happy hours, book tours, cycling clubs, and everything else our chapters were inventing. It was definitely no longer focused on drinking. We are out there to make sure wherever you live and whatever your interests, you can find or start a chapter that works for you. We want to make sure that whatever you're doing, however you're living, you're able to live liberally.

These past seven years taught me about our country, and about being liberal. It was clear to me what a liberal should be doing in New York City: we had to register voters, support candidates, attend forums. The experiences of our other chapters around the country have taught me to expand the vision of what a liberal is. A woman in Idaho had to write a letter to the editor of her local paper to argue that one could be a liberal and a god-fearing Christian, after her politics were denigrated in an editorial. Another woman in Natchez, Mississippi, had diffi-culty finding a bar where white and black Democrats would feel comfortable sharing a drink. For these communities, being liberal was more of a battle than it was to those of us in New York or San Francisco.

I also learned from our red-state friends that even the most conservative communities have ways that locals can live liberally. Des Moines, Iowa, has more than one lesbian bar active in supporting local social and political causes. Lincoln, Nebraska, has a thriving green market that would rival Union Square in New York. Laramie, Wyoming, is a hotbed of peace activists. In Savannah, Georgia, folks are fighting for more locally grown, sustainable school lunches.

Additionally, as Drinking Liberally evolved into Living Liberally, I realized how much more one could do to embody liberal values beyond voting and campaigning. I can consume food and entertainment that reflect my values. I can choose media, retail, and community resources free from corporate control.

I can also bring that spirit that first motivated Drinking Liberally into other walks of life. The spirit of creating and embracing a diverse community, of learning from each other, of forming social bonds that lead to collective action and progressive change, and of doing all this with a sense of fun along the way—these impulses can flow through how we work and play, learn and spend.

Across the United States, people are already Living Liberally— some intentionally, others without realizing it. If we start to recognize where these liberal impulses are in our everyday lives, and where we can take measures to live more liberally, then, step by step, we will create liberal communities, a liberal country, and a more liberal world.

That's not to say we're no longer Drinking Liberally. We still meet every Thursday, 7:30 PM onward, at the same dive bar on 9th Avenue between 44th and 45th streets. Pitchers have gone up a dollar in the past seven years. Hot dogs are still free. Come on by.

# CHAPTER 2
# LIVING LIBERALLY
## IN YOUR EVERY-DAY LIFE

*Of all the varieties of virtues,*
*liberalism is the most beloved.*
— ARISTOTLE

You wake up to your alarm clock playing National Public Radio, and you start your day. After twenty minutes of yoga, twenty more of Zen meditation, and a calm look through the *New York Times*, you have your Fair Trade latte and leave your home— powered half with solar energy, half with wind—to head off in your hybrid—no, make that your bicycle—to your nonprofit social service job.

You have woken up in Liberal America.

Seriously . . . who really has time for leisurely yoga and the *New York Times*? I don't have that many hours in my day, much less my morning. A solar-wind hybrid home? Is that even possible?

That morning routine may sound like a dream to you—or it may be your nightmare. Either way, it's not the typical liberal morning. I'm not sure if there is one typically liberal way to start your day . . . but there are easy steps to start your day off on the left foot.

Yes, I do like NPR; no, I don't do yoga; I don't drink lattes; my crowded NYC apartment is neither solar-nor wind-powered; and I take public transportation to work. Does that make me more or less liberal than the stereotype above? Not sure . . . but it is more real.

Here are some real ideas for **Waking Liberally:**

## Choose Your Morning News

Whether you wake up to a blaring alarm or to music, if you're like most people you pretty quickly switch on a radio or television. The voice helps ease you into the day . . . and may give you some insights into what's going on in the world.

Consciously deciding whose voice and views start your day is a good place to start your Liberal Morning. What you listen to, watch, or read helps set your mood. You could listen to DJs gossip about the previous night's reality TV, or you could listen to radio that will inform your conversations later in the day. Listening to NPR—yes, a stereotype, but a good one—offers you insights and information that may help you engage and influence the members of your car pool, coworkers at your water cooler, and family members at the dinner table. Good radio becomes a source of contagious conversation.

I emphasize "listening" over "watching" because there is something dangerous in that seductive, addictive drug called television. You might consider covering your television to lessen your impulse to just flick it on. Once you do, the hours drain away. Another good tactic is to leave magazines out and open around your house. Just as TV can suck you in, I hope that *The Nation* or *Mother Jones* can, too.

That said, if you do prefer television to radio, there are still choices you can make. You could choose local stations to become informed about your community or public television for coverage that tends to be less sensational than cable news. If you want a dose of fear and anger, start with Fox News, or switch off Fox and watch just about anything else to improve your morning.

If you do have time to read the paper or the news online, why not? Sadly, many of us are in too much of a rush . . . but reading is the best way to get a sense of the world, as you can skim and scan through various stories and synthesize them for yourself.

## Make Your Lunch

Breakfast starts your day, but think ahead to lunch. If you prepare lunch at home, it's a cost-saving move, and also spares your wastebasket, given how much trash each take-out meal produces. Use a reusable lunch bag for extra green points. Plus, make sure to compost to reduce and reuse your food waste.

Not everything is compostable, of course, so also know your recycling rules. Many municipalities remain mediocre when it comes to recycling. The best way you can help is by sorting properly so they don't have any excuse.

## Turn Off Your House

As you leave each morning for work, let your home take some time to rest. Shutting down your house for the day saves energy costs and sets a pattern of conscious, sustainable choices that will follow you through your day.

**15**
**16**

Why control the climate of an empty house? Turn off the AC or turn down the thermostat. Turn off lights. We all should have learned that one already.

**17**

Remember to unplug things that don't need to be left on. Unplug everything? Really? Well, no need to get obsessive. But the fact is that most appliances, televisions, even cell phone and laptop chargers continue to waste electricity when they're not being used. If you don't want to be the manic person who unplugs

**18**

her television every time she's not watching, consider surge protectors and power strips, which stop burning electricity in the off position.

**19**

You can make this easier if you use an Energy Hub. While we may be a few years away from these being common commercial products, the basic idea is appealing: you run all your appliances through this little device that helps turn them on and off in environmentally conscious and lifestyle-affirming ways. It can change your AC settings during the night, or get it cooling just before you come home. It will power down TVs and DVD players. It may even start your coffeemaker for you while you sleep . . .

**20**

Bigger picture: monitor your energy use to save waste and money. There are great groups like Earth Aid that monitor your use for you, offer you information on how much your neighbors are using, give you tips to reduce, and reward you (financially!) if you

**21**
**22**
**23**

reduce your use and beat out your neighbors. Make the switch to compact fluorescents and low-flow showerheads to start, and ask your power company about alternative energy. Most power companies will allow you to request your electricity come from wind power or other alternative sources. This creates a market for that energy, which will bring down the cost over time.

One more fun idea, as you're unplugging your phones and iPods

**24**

and carrying them off for the day: There are backpacks with

solar panels on them that build up enough current to charge your mobile devices while you're on the go. Buy one of those and you never run down, you save money and electricity, and you definitely start some conversations.

## Commute Liberally

Maybe you work from home, telecommuting in your PJs all day—what a way to save yourself some peace of mind, and save the planet your carbon emissions. No? Then maybe you get to bicycle to work, exercising while you head to the office. But in most places, that's just not practical.

Use public transportation when you can—what's more communal than mass transit? You literally share space with neighbors and strangers alike. But the reality is that many people have to drive. Furthermore, not everyone can afford a hybrid vehicle.

All is not lost: that's why the car pool was created. It creates a little community of fellow travelers who save fuel and money, look out for each other, and share news, stories, and the road.

You also save time: dedicated high-occupancy vehicle (HOV) or carpool lanes whisk you and your teammates along the fast track. Makes you want to advocate for more of those in your area . . .

Sure, people who go it alone have their own car, their own climate control, their own radio, their own schedule . . . and they'll sit in traffic a whole lot longer.

## Caffeinate Liberally

You may have noticed I skipped one critical step in the morning ritual: coffee. Worry not: if you're like me, you didn't get as far as a car pool without first stopping by the coffeepot. I saved this for the last of the morning rituals because our relationship to coffee is so sacred, it deserves its own section.

To the detriment of my health, my wallet, and at times my morals, I am a compulsive coffee drinker. So I want to make sure liberal values are percolating along with the grounds.

A few tips to make the most of your morning joe.

**31** **Brew your own.** Save money and packaging by making your own coffee, rather than stopping at the coffee shop along the way. You can even enjoy a cup while reading the *Times* and fill up another for the road. Which brings up a good point . . .

**32** **Use a travel mug.** A travel mug keeps the coffee going strong as you go long. And if you didn't have time to brew, or if you run low, you can go into a store and ask them to refill your mug, saving on yet another paper cup. Often, the cashier won't know what to charge you at first . . . but she'll figure it out. And if many more of us start carrying our own vessels, **33** we'll form a large enough group to start lobbying for discounts. After all, we're saving them money too.

**34** **Know your brew.** Make your own decisions about which coffee tastes best; but be aware of which labor and environmental practices would leave a bad taste in your mouth. Keep an eye out for **35** phrases like Fair Trade—it makes a big difference. Fair Trade coffee is sold by collectives of local farmers—the purchase rate is higher than they might otherwise receive, and the money is reinvested into their local communities. Another term to look for: shade grown, which means farmers **36** did not clear fields to cultivate coffee. Excessive clearing leads to erosion and decimates the health benefits of trees for our air and ecosystems. Coffee can eat up your insides physically . . . no need for it to do so morally.

**Make more than you need.** Wait, wait, wait . . . isn't producing too much wasteful, therefore un-green, ergo un-liberal? Well, it would be if we were throwing it out. But when you make more, you share more. Why not bring a travel mug to your carpool-mate (and maybe tomorrow, she'll bring one for you)? Or take a thermos to the office? We're a caffeine culture. . . . I'm not out to starve that addiction; I just want to make it a little more communal.

With a little more research, you'll find ways to liberalize your morning rituals. The government's Energy Star program is full of ideas for reducing consumption at your home. And I still remember reading *50 Simple Things You Can Do to Save the Earth* when I was in the single digits, and as a result diligently turning off the sink faucet as I brushed my teeth. I still do feel a little pang of guilt when I let water run in a trickle as I shave . . . a sign of how effective that book was getting into my subconscious more than twenty years ago.

Maybe twenty years from now, someone will need to explain to their kids why they brew so much coffee. . . .

## Who Are the People in Your Neighborhood?

Inside your house, most of what you do is about making progressive politics personal. The next thing you do each morning is enter the outside world—where progressive politics becomes public—where "you" and "I" become "we."

Even before you head to work—before you climb into your carpool vehicle, power up your hybrid, or hop on your bicycle—look around your home and ask the question sung by those great liberal Muppets on *Sesame Street*: "Who are the people in your neighborhood?"

42 43 Do you know your neighbors? Do you smile at them? Say hi? Know their names? Invite them over? I'm not just being nosy here. . . . I'm asking questions that are directly connected to your happiness.

There are studies that have demonstrated that happiness is contagious. When your neighbors are happy, it rubs off on you, and you become happy. That's good incentive to know who is on your block. It's not enough just to be near them, though . . . you need to know their names and what's going on in their lives. So, say hello for a healthier life.

Look around: who are the people in your neighborhood, the people who you meet as you're walking down the street? Do you even walk down the street? Or do you depart from an attached garage in a car with windows closed, AC on, and Neighbor Radar turned off? Do you see your neighbors and wave, or has the high fence between your homes successfully hidden you from all contact?

My mother recalls growing up in an old neighborhood in East New York, an area of Brooklyn that, at the time, had a large Jewish population. Kids played in the streets, but they were safe. Both my grandparents worked, but my mom wasn't unsupervised. 44 All the neighbors kept an eye on each other. The grandmothers on the block sat on their stoops and shouted to the kids when they were being too rambunctious. And the kids—rather than ignoring some old lady yelling at them—listened. Why? Because that old lady knew their parents.

This community supervision is celebrated by Jane Jacobs in her book *The Death and Life of Great American Cities*. Incidental policing provides a sense of safety. It's also self-perpetuating: if those old ladies needed anything, the kids would be there to help.

45

There's something else wonderfully liberal that happens in the best of neighborhoods: people are exposed to the diversity of other families. Sure, my mom's block felt Jewish, but in the spray fountains of the playground one block over, Jewish, black, and Italian kids ran around together.

You don't need a scene out of a Neil Simon play to have a good neighborhood. Just look around for the features that create shared space . . . literally the "common ground" that can help turn strangers into neighbors and neighbors into friends. These democratic spaces allow — even encourage — people to meet and mingle, share concerns and hopes, discuss community affairs, plan events, and extend invitations. And no, these magical spaces I discuss are nothing more remarkable than that spray fountain in Brooklyn in the 1950s.

**Visit your neighborhood parks.** Parks are true community assets. They help us breathe easier; trees and green pathways contribute to public health. They give children a place to play, seniors a way to get outside, and families and neighbors a destination to visit together. All over the country, neighborhood parks are the easiest way to create common ground.

46

Backyards are terrific . . . but inherently private. You have your swing set for your kids. Your children aren't asked to share, they don't learn to socialize with new friends. Not that you should never hang out in your backyard, but give your public park a chance.

**47**   **Play in your area playgrounds.** Playgrounds, in addition to parks, fulfill this liberal ideal. The first public playgrounds were built in New York City at the start of the nineteenth century. They were specifically situated in the city's poorest, most crowded areas, usually populated by immigrants, to ensure that children got out for exercise, fresh air, and a good dose of civic engagement.

Now, the importance of play is a real public policy concern and not only for the poorest communities. The impact of play and playgrounds is so widely understood that advocacy groups are increasingly succeeding in making access to playgrounds a public commitment. The organization KaBOOM!, which builds playgrounds—often in needy areas like post-Katrina

**48** New Orleans—has been getting mayors to sign on to their "Play Cities" agenda, part of which assures playgrounds and play opportunities in close proximity to every child.

Of course, creating that prevalence of playgrounds and parks requires space. In cities, open space can be a tight commodity, and in small towns and suburbs, it still takes a lot of resources to create, preserve, maintain, and program shared spaces. Conse-

**49** quently, local representatives need to be reminded again and again how important these areas are, and, sometimes, we can't just leave it to our public officials.

**50**   **Visit a community garden.** All across the country, citizens are finding creative solutions to open-space shortages. Community gardens are often born in vacant lots. Sometimes, they begin with the permission of an owner or city agency that has no use for the lot. Sometimes, communities just take over abandoned areas, clean them up, and claim them for public use. The New York–based "Green Guerillas" used the latter method to create dozens of such gardens.

Without public funding, these gardens are truly supported by the "public"—that is, the public citizens who create self-governing methods to maintain these spaces. In many cases, they really do become gardens, growing vegetables and flowers. They provide opportunities for people to grow their own organic produce and learn more about what "organic" means. At the very least, they also provide the opportunity for people to enjoy open space that they collectively created.

**Create a play street.** Play streets are another communal vision for how to open shared spaces in your neighborhood. In New York City, this phenomenon has closed down city blocks over the summer for decades, giving congested neighborhoods the outdoor space they need . . . right outside their front doors. Like the streets my mom remembers, or the streets I grew up on in small-town New Jersey, these avenues become places to play team sports and board games, learn from each other, or just hang out.

In the summer of 2009, the *New York Times* profiled one such play street in the Bronx, a street that had run for thirty-three summers, largely thanks to the perseverance of one local woman who insisted on it and organized her neighbors to support it. But she couldn't do it alone. To close the street, she needed 51 percent of the residents of the block to sign a petition. How's that for the benefits of knowing your neighbors?

You don't have to live in a city or push yourself into public parks to develop bonds with your neighbors. Gated communities make it difficult to feel the democratic flow of different people, income levels, and backgrounds. Life in a McMansion may mean you never even pass your neighbors on the street. Wherever you live, you can at least take some steps to answer the question, "Who are the people in your neighborhood?" and then ask a second question, oft-intoned by that great liberal, Mr. Rogers: "Won't you be my neighbor?"

# Left Detour

**Mr. Rogers.** Fred Rogers, the beloved children's television host who asked us to make believe and to open our imaginations and our welcoming spirits and in an unassuming cardigan taught us how to be a good neighbor, passed away in February 2003. A few weeks later, on what would have been his seventy-fifth birthday, March 20, I sent around an e-mail to everyone in my address list letting people know it was "Won't You Be My Neighbor Day," a tribute to Mr. Rogers that you celebrated by doing neighborly acts while wearing sneakers and a cardigan.

I had made the holiday up; I thought someone should. I wore a zip-up sweatshirt that day (I didn't own a cardigan), but, as far as I knew, the day never caught on. That said, a cursory Google search reveals that Family Communications (fci.org) continues to promote an annual event of the same name and even offers a "Caring Neighbor Checklist" with such recommendations as "Share a Hug," "Volunteer at a Senior Center," and "Visit Your Local Library."

I'd love to believe my e-mail and lone celebration was forwarded to them. More likely, I should recognize that if you have a good idea, chances are someone else had it, too. I'm just glad they saw it through.

Want to invite your neighbors into your life? Or inject yourself into theirs a little bit more? Here are a few ideas that don't take much time or ask you to change your life too much. Each action helps cultivate a liberal landscape, one in which we embrace the idea: We better get to know one another since we're all in this together. And that would make Mr. Rogers proud.

**Sit on your porch.** Yes, inside is climate controlled and the remote is only an arm's length away. But you already know what you'll see if you stay inside . . . who knows what you may find when you turn outward? It makes it more likely you'll see your neighbors and they'll see you. It will increase your appreciation of the rhythm of your street. People around you feel safer and more welcome (assuming you don't grimace at them), thereby lowering those barriers so that happiness can be as contagious as possible.

If you're in a city, fear not. The stoop counts. I've met friends on my stoop—one of them is now on our block association and organizes movie screenings in our local playground. All because I was sitting out front rather than out back or up on my fire escape. Oh, and because she said hello. Which brings us to point two:

**Say hi to your neighbors.** Sounds obvious. But do you do it? If you're like me, there are days when you just want to keep your head down. You're a little scared: if you say hi, next thing you know you'll have to say, "How are you?" Then you're making small talk . . . and that can sometimes be annoying.

However, think about what you can get for those few seconds of annoyance. You might make a new friend. Or recruit someone to a neighborhood association (or be recruited yourself). You create a connection with someone who will hold a set of your keys, or help you carry your groceries, or take in your mail while you're gone. Yes, saying hello is never just saying hello . . . it's a slippery slope into full-fledged community. But you know what? I bet it will cause you more smiles than aggravation in the end.

Although, if a few moments of conversation is too much for you, you're going to hate the next idea:

**Invite your neighbors over.** Whoa, whoa, whoa. My home is my castle. The point of a castle is to keep people out. And if I want to interact with neighbors, isn't that what parks are for? You spent pages telling us to go to our local playgrounds . . . now you want us to stay inside?

Realistically, you're not going to spend your whole life outside. Winter comes. And there's a lot of quality time that is better served inside: meals, games, TV. Yes . . . TV. I'm a liberal, but I'm not a Puritan!

Personally, I don't cook, so I'd be a hypocrite if I encouraged everyone to invite neighbors over for a meal (though I would gladly accept such invitations). But there is plenty I do in my own home that could be shared with my neighbors . . . and would even be improved by my neighbors' presence.

I like chess. I can't play alone. Would my neighbor enjoy a game? I should ask.

I love charades, celebrity, salad bowl, and all those other games when groups of people shout out answers at each other's absurd clues and gestures. If I shouted guesses at myself, that may be too easy . . . and a little crazy. However, if I'm inviting other friends over anyway, why not knock next door? The worst that happens is that Duane (my next-door neighbor) will say no. The best? He may be able to mime "*To Kill a Mockingbird*" or "Ronald Reagan" really well.

Here's an even wackier idea: invite neighbors over to watch TV. People do this with sporting events all the time . . . how about with the news? Or a good comedy? Or even better: comedy news? *The Daily Show* is a dish best served shared—when you can laugh together . . . and discuss it afterward.

It may be weird to invite neighbors over to watch the Jim Lehrer *NewsHour*, but *The Daily Show* is entertainment. And—it's short. You'll only be entertaining guests for half an hour.

You invite them over for *The Daily Show*, and maybe they'll invite you over to see some of those programs on premium cable that you can't afford.

Now, what does swapping TV times have to do with living liberally?

★ It makes television a shared resource. You've just socialized HBO.

★ It transforms a very inward, private activity into a public, shared one . . . you can discuss and debate.

★ It creates community. What starts with watching TV together can become attending a community meeting or organizing a letter-writing campaign. You start organizing a community and before you know it, you're—gasp!—a community organizer.

Bonus: buy a projector, and turn TV shows into big-screen experiences. It's just more fun that way.

**Make enough food to share.** As a non-cook, this is a little outside of my skill set. But several times I've been the beneficiary of neighbors who have knocked on my door, announced that they made too much food, and asked if I would like to share it with them.

Did they really overcook, or were they looking for an excuse to reach out? Either way, the result was the same: I was fed. I also developed a sense of warmth for these people I passed in the halls each day. It made me want to help them—carry bags up the stairs, or check in on their family's health. It made me a better neighbor.

The quickest way to my heart was indeed through my stomach.

60 **Share an internet connection and wi-fi router** with your neighbor. You know you want high-speed connectivity at home ... but why shoulder the cost alone? This becomes one more resource that
61 you and neighbors can share. If you feel really liberal, leave it unlocked and make someone else very happy.

62 **Think public.** As you make choices about schooling, recreation, and resources outside your home, consider the public option. When you participate in shared programs and venues, you meet people in your community, come to see issues from their perspectives, and begin to share needs and goals.

This is one of the appeals of public parks—it also extends to public recreation centers. In many cities, where there are not municipal recreation options, the local YMCAs (or their equivalent) serve this role. Many of them offer sliding-scale memberships, so nobody gets turned away. They are more affordable than private fitness centers and create an environment where you and your family will meet people you might not encounter on your street or at your workplace.

This is also true, of course, of one of our country's greatest assets: our public schools. They are our best hope for teaching democracy. They give everyone a level playing field, encourage kids of different backgrounds to meet, and remind a community that all its members are invested in a single resource.

There are plenty of reasons why private schools can be attractive. You might be in an area where the public schools are underfunded or where drug activity gets in the way of learning. You may want your children to have a religious education, or they may have special needs that a private school can meet. I went to a private high school, and had an incredible experience; I also know that it allowed me privileges that not everyone shared. It's a complicated question, because parents want what's best for their children, as they should. Staying invested in the public school is often the way to improve it.

Every family will have to make its own choice, but at least think about public schools. Try them out. You'll discover devoted teachers and the potential for strong community bonds, and your kids deserve to be part of this great experience of democracy.

As you're thinking about public facilities, you can also think about public health. The costs of health care are overwhelming and heavily tax us all. Fortunately, we can protect ourselves, prevent disease among our neighbors, and reduce our communal health care costs at the same time. Get vaccinations to prevent the spread of disease; you might not be at risk yourself, but you do not want to carry diseases to more vulnerable members of society. Don't smoke—not only does it hurt you, but it hurts those around you and incurs incredible health costs down the road. Pick up trash in your community. Don't go to work when you're sick. Preventing contagion improves everyone's health and saves everyone money. (One more reason to advocate for paid sick days for all employees.) Thinking about the public good is an important way of living for others, not just for yourself.

> 63

> 64

> 65 66

> 67

## How Large Is Your 'Hoodprint?

Over the past couple years, you've probably heard about your "carbon footprint." That's shorthand for how much greenhouse

gas you are personally responsible for, directly or indirectly. So
you take steps to reduce your carbon footprint on our planet.

More recently, food activists, concerned about access to healthy,
local foods and about the impact of our food system on the environment, have asked us to mind our "foodprint"—the ecological
impact of production and delivery of the food we eat.

Has anyone ever defined a "'hoodprint"—the boundaries of
the neighborhood (physical or virtual) in which you live? I'm a
global, cosmopolitan, big-city guy, so I'm not saying you should
stick close to home all the time, but there is something nice about
the grocer you recognize, or the mail carrier who calls you by
name. There's strength in a community where you can walk to
school, a park, and a movie theater. There are smart environmental and financial consequences to a walk/bike lifestyle as
well as societal advantages that are harder to quantify.

Are there ways you can shrink your 'hoodprint? Can you shop at
a local mom-and-pop rather than drive out to the big-box store?
Can you get some pleasure attending a local minor-league game,
or seeing a show at the local community center? No need to cut
out Major League and Broadway altogether, but are there ways
you can take from—and in doing so, invest in—your community?
The subsequent chapters are filled with reasons to go local . . .
and in doing so, shrink your 'hoodprint.

Though he didn't use the term 'hoodprint, one social scientist
first made me think about the concept. Actually, he's a friend:
David Alpert, one of the partners who took Living Liberally
national, and the publisher of Greater Greater Washington, a
website devoted to discussions of smart city planning.

He once wrote about his friend who lived in a small town—
population about 8,000. His friend had lived there for a number
of years, and his parents had worked there when he was growing

up. He saw people he knew while he walked down the street. He inquired after them, and they checked in on how his family was doing. His supermarket, movie theater, favorite diner and bar, clinic and playground were all within walking distance, and he knew by name many of the people who served him coffee and eggs . . . and they knew how he wanted them.

This sounded familiar, because it sounded a little like the town where I grew up, Highland Park, New Jersey. It was a small walkable town, over the river from New Brunswick, the larger "city" where Rutgers University is based. In Highland Park, I could walk to my friends' homes at an early age, walk to school, and walk to the store. I knew my friends' parents, and in many cases their grandparents, and they knew mine, because some of the kids I knew in preschool, I knew through all of childhood. It was a town where you could play in the street (as well as the backyard).

So I knew what David was talking about. Turned out, though, I knew better than I had realized. David's essay had a twist: the friend was me, and the small town was Hell's Kitchen, on the bustling, crowded west side of Manhattan, just blocks from Times Square and the Broadway theater district. He'd looked up the census data for my few square blocks—and realized I'd created a small-town feel, with neighbors, familiar strangers, regular haunts.

I'd gotten my 'hoodprint to eight blocks.

I live in the center of a big city, and yet some days don't venture more than a few streets from my home. There are the environmental savings of not driving and the convenience of the tight radius. Then there is the real benefit: in a world where more and more people say they feel alienated from neighbors, where people build walls between themselves and others, I feel like I have a home. And that's Living Liberally.

# Living Liberally in the Larger World

Being neighborly is at the core of being liberal—but it is not the exclusive domain of liberals. A conservative all-white neighborhood might have good community spirit, but is a far cry from the diverse, inclusive world a liberal envisions.

We have to extend our thinking. If we see value in creating a connection with our neighbors, we should see the similar worth in our neighborhood and the next neighborhood working together, to share resources, help each other out, and tackle problems bigger than either neighborhood could handle on its own. This is why towns need to work together, why states seek solutions to larger problems through the federal government, and why different countries ultimately recognize we need to collaborate across borders.

Additionally, the truth of the world in which we live is that we cannot choose a life shaped only by other people and forces we select. A racist may wish to live in an all-white enclave, but that is not the reality of the arc of history (nor should it be). I may enjoy my eight-block 'hoodprint, but everything from the cost of my food to the quality of my air, from the entertainment I enjoy to the traffic on my street, is influenced by far more than that parcel I call home.

We are all subject to the decisions of people we may never meet and to conditions created by choices made outside our neighborhood. Similarly, we affect the lives of others every day. That is why when we recognize "we are all in this together," we do not only mean "our block" or "our race" or "our religion." In a complex, interconnected world, an approach that embraces diversity and encourages everyone to think about a greater good is not just pleasant, but necessary.

So when you <u>attend your Block Association</u> or <u>help a neighbor with a chore</u>, you are taking steps to create a society where we look out for each other; the key is then taking those same impulses beyond the neighborhood you see and the people you know, and applying those same values to the larger world.

On the surface, this may not seem radical—or even overtly political. However, if you look around our culture, you see many trends that show we are not looking out for each other and are, instead, living for ourselves alone:

★ The popularity of larger cars, such as SUVs, which have countered efforts at fuel-efficiency so these tank-like vehicles can fulfill a fantasy of "owning the road."

★ The decrease, over the past half-century, in participation in civic associations and community social events, coupled with the increase in insular television consumption.

★ The prevalence of gated communities with isolated mansions and private security forces that prevent the natural flow of commerce, people, and ideas.

These patterns of wanting one's own control, privilege, and separation come at the expense of community and the environment, make it easier to segregate oneself from people who are different, and allow one to escape from engaging in larger social issues.

If you look around, you will see choices we make that suggest we are *not* living for one another. That mind-set then seeps into our public discourse, and many of our toughest political questions divide those who believe we should care for one another and those who believe we must only care for ourselves.

**Climate Change.** When you're all in the same boat, nobody ignores the leak. It's only when you have your personal yacht that you can ignore the ship sinking next to you. If we were all invested in the fortunes of those around us, would anyone spend their time and money denying the impact of global warming? We would be working hard to tackle climate change in order to prevent disastrous water shortages and social unrest that might be the result of inaction. The only folks who have reason to fight action are companies looking after their short-term bottom line ahead of the common good.

74

**Health care.** Shouldn't one of the signs of a great country be its ability to support the health of our fellow citizens? Yet, opponents of universal coverage call it "big-government, socialized medicine." There are economic costs to all of us when people are unable to afford health insurance. They often miss out on preventative care, and end up in worsening situations by the time they turn to public hospitals. These become real costs to all of us: in the care they receive later in their illness, in the loss of healthy workers to our economy. Beyond the bottom line, though, there is the moral question: why should anyone die because they cannot get care? We would not accept that in our household or in our neighborhood—why accept it anywhere?

75

**Immigration.** Would you imagine people arguing against providing education for children of immigrants if we really believed we were in this together? You don't ask your new neighbor for a passport before helping them carry in bags of groceries or letting them into a local park. Why would that change for their children's ability to get an education and become contributing members of our larger society? When we agree that we are better off in a world where we all succeed, we not only feel a moral and humane obligation to those around us

76

regardless of their citizenship, but realize that undereducated children would be a larger social problem than opening our schools to new students.

**Estate Tax.** This tax only affected the wealthiest few percent of our country, returning a portion of their estate to the public good at the time of their death, acknowledging that personal wealth is accumulated with the support of public infrastructure. Conservatives rebranded it the "death tax." They convinced middle-class people that it would affect them, which was largely not the case; that it would leave their kids with nothing, which was never true; and that it was "their money, they earned it"— with no regard to how society's investment in infrastructure, regulations, and stability had helped them earn "their" money. They decimated the estate tax and effectively exacerbated wealth disparity in America. If we were interested in what's best for the greater good, we would support the estate tax as a fair, necessary measure.

[77]

**Progressive Taxation.** We say "taxes" like they are a bad thing. Yet, they help pay for the safety of our food, water, and air, the usability of our roads and transit, the protection of our country, the functionality of our courts, and the depth of our scientific inquiry. Supreme Court Justice Oliver Wendell Holmes once opined, "Taxes are what we pay for a civilized society." Less famously, my childhood friend's father once said, "Stop whining and pay your taxes." Why should we approach tax day with dread, when that is what invests in our country, shared fortune, and future? We should cheer on progressive taxation. We are all in this together—and that means we all need to invest together.

[78]

A common conservative argument is to accuse good ideas of being "socialist." The very word sets off alarm bells. Americans have a gut reflex against the word. Is that because of decades of facing off against the "Evil Empire"? (Reagan's words, not mine . . . I've always found Russians to be quite hospitable.) Is it because of our Horatio Alger "pull yourself up by your boot-straps" American ideal? Or is it because political leaders are so scared of certain words that once the right wing calls something "socialist," it becomes too hard to defend the idea?

They call expanding health care a "socialist plan to create government-run health care." They accuse environmental regulations, school funding, and progressive tax structures of being "socialist" because they would require our government to supervise more regulations and invest more in national infra-structure.

What they object to as "socialist" are services that are "shared," "supported by all," "serving all," and often "structured by govern-ment." The irony is that there are already many great aspects of the American way of life that fit that description.

While there are pervasive conservative trends in America, we are not ultimately a go-it-alone, every-man-for-himself society. There are strong liberal instincts in America as well. These liberal tendencies live in many of our country's great institutions. We don't call them "liberal" per se, but they embody those values. They pool our resources to deliver strong, public services. They serve all of us, not discriminating by our income, race, neigh-borhood, or nationality. They are services often strengthened by our participation, frequently benefiting from the democratic engagement of those they serve. These institutions invest in the common good and are proof that we are better off when we live, work, and contribute together.

What are some examples of these shared services for the common good?

79  Let's start with our National Park Service. There are vast tracts of land throughout our country preserved for the public's

enjoyment: for our recreation, for beautiful vistas that leave us breathless, for opportunities to learn about a wild America that pre-dated us all.

Admission costs are kept low. Paths are maintained. Rangers are present, friendly, and helpful. Families enjoy unique experiences that go beyond what they'd find in their hometown and surpass what many of them could afford if they had to fly to a remote destination or rent an expensive hotel.

Our "Big Government" has succeeded in giving us "socialized" national parks.

You don't have to head off to the national parks in Wyoming, the land of Dick Cheney, or Alaska, the land of Sarah Palin, to find such "socialized" programs at work. Shared programs are at the core of our communities everywhere. Just look around your hometown. . .

**Firefighters.** In a great bit, Laughing Liberally comedian Lee Camp jokes about what it would be like if fire departments worked like health care: Before they put out your fire, they have to check your insurance; you may not get full coverage; maybe your fire was a preexisting condition.

80

We salute and celebrate our firefighters for a reason, and it's not because they only help those who pay or lecture people about "putting your fire out by your bootstraps." They are a community good. In many areas, you can volunteer for your fire department. Volunteer firefighters embody the spirit that we all have to look out for each other.

81

**Police.** Do you have to use the "government-run" police force? No—you can opt out of that "public option" and hire your own private security, which many wealthier communities do. Most Americans see a value in a police force that works for everyone.

82

A private security firm would be happy enough to push a problem along to another neighborhood. Public safety, inherently, cannot be private or segregated; it must protect us all.

83 **Libraries.** Would you accuse your local librarian of being a communist? We have private bookstores, of course, but still value our libraries and do not consider them unfair competition. Pooling knowledge and making information available to the public is good for society.

84 In addition to using your local library, lending a hand and donating to your book drive are liberal acts: actions that support a communal resource that prizes community over commerce.

85 **Schools.** Unless we're all going to send our kids to private schools, we need this "government program." As with most of the institutions listed, it's not enough to pay taxes and let it ride. Schools need parental and community involvement. School systems that shut out parents are rightly criticized. When schools serve as a resource for parents who want to engage in their 86 87 child's education, they're at their best. Join a PTA. Offer to be 88 a guest speaker. Open your business for a class trip.

89 **Food pantries.** Why would you donate canned goods to people you may not even know? Because you—and your church—believe that it is important to look out for the less fortunate. This is an example that isn't necessarily government-run; often places of worship embody liberal characteristics.

90 **Soup kitchens.** You would never ask why those in need of a meal don't go to a restaurant instead. The volunteers who staff kitchens and shelters are doing tremendous work. Don't just take that from a political lefty; every religious institution in the country would call it the "Lord's work" to feed and house the hungry and homeless.

We learn our political beliefs through the interactions we have and the conversations that lead us in new directions. I would find it hard to believe that someone who worked extensively in a soup kitchen didn't come away believing the people he or she served deserved a chance to make the most of their lives. When you don't talk to homeless people, it's easy to detach from them—they are the "other," unlike us, uninterested in working or pulling themselves together. When you talk to them over a meal, you can't help but realize they are human, like you or me.

Does that mean you'll believe in our current welfare system as it works? Not necessarily. Policies and programs are flawed. However, you will come away believing that there should be services that give these folks a chance and the support they need to find new opportunities. And whether or not you believe those services should be government supported, you're already on the right track of knowing that we do have to look out for our fellow citizens.

**Public access TV.** As goofy as it can be (and justifiably lampooned in *Wayne's World*), public access is one more institution that engages community creativity and delivers back some community good. It teaches skills, builds self-esteem and confidence, promotes community dialogue, and usually does so without commercialization.

**Seed banks.** Of this list, seed banks are the least likely sentinel of socialism to reach your neighborhood, not yet as common as libraries and food pantries. The idea is to create a library of seeds—so if you want to grow vegetables or flowers, you use the seeds collectively shared and catalogued. At the end of the season, you return seeds for others to use. It's beautifully self-perpetuating, encourages curiosity, and is a surprising opportunity to pool natural resources.

What makes it truly radical, though, is how these banks cut out agribusiness. There is an "Agricultural Industrial Complex," and they want to own seeds. It sounds absurd . . . but these companies genetically modify seeds to resist weather or disease and patent those creations. So, most seeds you buy are "designer seeds"—and believe it or not, they remain the intellectual property of the companies. If you want to share your seeds, they could legally stop you. This isn't just theoretical . . . agribusiness has done it.

Regardless of the legal arguments, something just seems wrong about that. And seed banks are an institution out to set it right.

All of these examples demonstrate two points:

1) Collectivist institutions are all around us despite the stamping and shouting that we can't have "socialized government programs."

2) It's not enough that they exist. We need to engage with them. We need to improve them and contribute to them. Using our shared resources is a hallmark of a liberal lifestyle; supporting these resources is truly living like a liberal.

You drive on big-government roads to get to a collectivist post office and people in your family enjoy government-run programs like Social Security, Medicare, and Head Start. It was the "greater good" spirit that led to government involvement in supervising safety in food, water, air, and airlines, and in cleaning up Superfund toxic sites. When you stop to think about how much you benefit from a government motivated by an "all in this together" attitude, you don't need to declare yourself a socialist. Just declare yourself a liberal.

# CHAPTER 3

# WORKING LIBERALLY

> *A liberal is a man too broadminded*
> *to take his own side in a quarrel.*
> —ROBERT FROST

Here's a wild-eyed vision: a workplace where employees could dedicate some of their time at the office to independent projects. They are not told what to do with every moment; rather, their supervisors trust that if given the latitude to experiment, these employees will come up with something good for the company.

Imagine if this were not the only flexibility in their workday. They can come in when they want, as long as they stay late as well. They may wear what they want. Plus, they are well compensated.

What if the company provided, in addition to generous wages, free meals—lunch every day, and dinner for employees who stay late? Periodically, the office would close and take everyone to the movies.

What could make this dreamier? Jars full of jelly beans and coolers of refreshing fruit drinks around the workplace . . . all for free . . .

If these ideas seem crazy . . . then Google is the craziest company I've ever heard of. Google—not the verb that it's become, but the business behemoth that has changed our lives—has a workplace culture that would seem anathema to the button-up world of traditional offices. "Button-up" most definitely wouldn't apply, given that there's no dress code. There is a casual, comfortable feel that earns their California compound the description "campus."

It's almost like they want to make their employees happy.

Their dining halls are well stocked and meals are well known for being tasty and healthy. So their programmers—who are, after all, human and love free food—stay late. At their Mountainview campus, they even have a mobile dentist and mobile barber come periodically.

Now, it's not all altruistic. These services keep employees from having to make appointments and save them trips "off-campus," thus maximizing the time they spend contributing to the company. And they make the staff feel some gratitude, even loyalty. They have social outings and barbecues together, and, if you haven't heard, the company is making money.

It's not that Google is an inherently liberal company. Google sometimes behaves very liberally—it challenged the Bush administration over privacy issues—and sometimes less so, as when it worked with the Chinese government to censor web searches. Al Gore may be a longtime advisor, but Google is also a growing enterprise that has had its own examples of stamping out competition.

As a workplace, though, it offers ideas on how to build a sense of community, allow flexibility, encourage creativity, and respect its employees.

It doesn't require a world-renowned brand name to create this type of work environment. There are some steps that any employee could advocate for and any employer could implement to create an environment that is working liberally.

**Get your office recycling.** Everyone buys into it at this point, but not every commercial establishment knows how to do it. Learning the rules and making it easy saves money, reduces waste, and sets a good example.

96

**Make energy-saving improvements.** Most people know about lightbulb savings: buy efficient bulbs, install motion-activated lights in restrooms and closets, turn off lights at night. How about bathroom improvements: invest in low-flush toilets and urinals, hand driers instead of paper towels, and timed faucets, all of which save electricity and water and can improve public health? Or institute policies for turning off computers at night?

97 98 99 100 101 102 103 104

**Improve the kitchen.** Many offices assume you'll just eat out (or some assume you won't eat at all). Having a functional kitchen cuts down on your lunch costs and may also increase your productivity since you don't have to run to the gourmet deli down the block. This means more than having a refrigerator (which, by the way, should be an energy-efficient fridge). The kitchen needs to invite the staff to use it. Stock dishware to reduce waste and develop a system for cleaning the dishes. Have real utensils and provide common condiments and other frequently used items like milk for cereal.

105 106 107 108

And by all means, invest in a coffeemaker. I would reduce my own personal trash, expenses, and waste of time if there were always a pot of coffee brewing and I didn't need to run down the street.

109

**Get rid of the water cooler.** OK, water cooler conversation is important . . . it's often the best place to engage colleagues. But we don't actually need a water cooler to do it.

Bottled water is bad business. They take regular water. They truck it over many miles. Then they sell it to you, even though your water is fine to begin with. This creates waste, pollution, and, in some areas, water shortages. A water cooler is better than individually bottled water, but it's time to fight the aqua-industrial complex.

Unsure how you feel about tap water? Convince your office to invest in a filtering container or a filter that attaches to the faucet. Do your research, and you will find the cost savings come quickly.

**Relax the dress code.** If you work in a formal office, chances are that on your way to work on a hot day, you can't wait to get inside. You're overdressed for the heat, and you're in need of another shower after you crowd into public transportation or hop off your bicycle. The reason you're excited to get inside is because your office is blasting AC: drawing electricity, spewing pollutants, and generally wasting resources.

What if people could dress comfortably? Allowing staff to dress down has enabled businesses to relax the climate control. It saves money for the business and allows people to feel more at home . . . at work.

**Create avenues for staff feedback.** Every office will benefit from its staff feeling a sense of ownership—and that comes from including staff in discussions and decisions. If you work some-place, you should feel invested in it, and you have a perspective that should be valued. Whether a committee structure or a feedback box, there should be some mechanism by which management hears from its team.

**Provide flex time.** Why do you arrive at nine and leave at five? Is it so you have something in common with the Dolly Parton song? Or is it because everyone assumes you should?

115

Working the same hours as everyone else can have its advantages: it makes meetings easier to coordinate, and the office saves resources by only being open certain hours.

There are drawbacks. You all commute during the busiest hours of the day, adding time to your travel and maybe increasing the expense of your peak-hour tolls and train tickets. It also means someone who might moonlight at a night job is working the same hours as someone anxious to get home to be with their kids after school. Why shouldn't the mom or dad come in earlier and leave earlier, while the part-time DJ rolls in, fresher, later in the morning?

Technology makes this more possible. People can telecommute more easily or join meetings outside of their regular hours. And this "flex" approach to scheduling is making workers happier and more productive.

**Dedicate a staff lounge.** Wait—this place is called "work," so shouldn't we be working here? Most of your workspace is aimed at your job . . . but you don't sit at a desk all day. You go out for meals, hover in the kitchen, linger over the water cooler (or its enviro-friendly replacement).

116

A comfortable space for the staff facilitates the opportunity to turn your coworkers from fellow drones to potential friends. And since you tossed your water cooler, you need someplace to talk about the TV shows from the night before.

**Allow independent time.** What if 10–20 percent of your work hours were unstructured? You wouldn't have an assignment,

117

but you'd be at work . . . and whatever you worked on would be contributed to the company.

Would you innovate something new for your department, or come up with a new project your business should be involved in? Would you dream up a new marketing scheme, build a company Facebook page, or imagine some cost-saving measures? Would you conjure ideas for greening your workplace and research low-flow toilets?

Businesses need innovation from the people who know the businesses best and are invested in their success. If companies want innovation, they have to create room for it.

**Organize staff outings.** Sure, you have an office holiday party. But do you leave early on summer days for your office soft-ball team? Or go as a group on the first day a new movie is released? Building community with your coworkers is like building community anywhere: it leads to greater investment in each other's lives, respect for each other, and ultimately makes you better organized as you push to liberalize your workplace further. Seemingly silly measures like getting off early to go picnic together make your business stronger.

You may not do all of these ideas right off the bat, but starting with any of them is a good beginning. By the way, if people laugh at these ideas as silly, hippie pipe dreams, just ask if that means they do not want to become the next Google.

## Organizing Liberally

Jonah had worked at a major telecommunications company for years. He wasn't proud of it. He wasn't ashamed of it. It was his job; it wasn't his life. He had a social life and loved to read and talk about theater and arts and ideas with whomever he could find at his local coffee shop.

Then the 2004 election came around. Like many Americans, for the first time Jonah felt motivated to get involved. He began to volunteer for a campaign for the first time since he'd been in college in the late seventies. He spent evenings making phone calls and took weekend trips to Pennsylvania.

But there were still those eight hours a day, five days a week that he had to spend at work. So he decided to make the most use of his time, and he started engaging his coworkers in political discussions.

He looked around and saw smart, able people who were not giving a second thought to the larger political world, or their potential to have an impact on it. So he started asking them about their politics. It startled them, because nobody at the office much talked with each other unless they had to. When it wasn't business, it was small talk. But Jonah asked them what they thought of current events. More frequently, he told them what he thought. Unapologetically and unasked, he shared his opinions.

More than once he found himself in an animated diatribe in the office kitchen, confronting people who hadn't even disagreed with him . . . they probably hadn't said much of anything. They all knew better than to talk politics with Jonah.

Jonah does not regret how extreme he was getting. "My goal," he said, "wasn't to convince them. They weren't willing to have a conversation, how could I convince them of anything? My goal was to at least make them stop and think. I wanted them to say, 'Hey, what's Jonah so worked up about?' and reflect on the issues. I wanted to make them a little uncomfortable."

I like Jonah a lot. However, this section is not about becoming Jonah. In fact, in some ways, this is about *not* being Jonah. You can bring progressive political views into your work life in ways that make you comfortable and fulfilled and make your coworkers comfortable as well.

There are plenty of places to start that can make your work experience—whatever it is—more communal, more conscientious, and more reflective of your beliefs. Usually, your efforts in this direction will be more successful if you can bring some people along with you.

When I was graduating from college, there was a movement to sign on to the "green pledge." It didn't ask you to dedicate your life to a nonprofit field; it understood that people would move into all industries. Whatever discipline you joined, there was room for you to carry your values and consider the environmental and human rights impact of your work. We signed a pledge: "I pledge to explore and take into account the social and environmental consequences of any job I consider and will try to improve these aspects of any organizations for which I work."

Beyond the pledge, though, how do you make this real? Even if you are not working in a "green industry," is there room for you to liberalize your work experience?

You want your business to be a better political, social, and environmental actor in the larger world. First, though, start locally . . . by liberalizing your own office. The ideas above are a place to start. Some are simple pitches on environmental grounds; others pose greater challenges to how an office operates. Begin with the simple ones, get a feel for how to make change within your workplace, and it will be a natural next step to push your business to become more responsible on all fronts.

Excited by these ideas? Or dreaming up new innovations of your own? Whatever you're looking to accomplish—small, or large, in how your workplace operates, how your employers treat employees, or how your business relates to the world—you'll need to follow three simple steps: Advocate, Engage, Organize.

**Advocate.** You may not be the person who decides what bulbs to use, but if you know how to use the internet, you can make a really strong case for making the switch. You have the ability to research greener business practices and bring them to the powers-that-be. You don't want to make a demand every day, but if you smartly advocate your case, you'll have a greener workplace in no time. [121]

> **Research.** Whether it's asking for recycling or getting the company to ditch the water cooler in favor of a water filter, start by knowing the facts. Find out the environmental benefits and the financial costs. Look up other businesses that have done the same, so that you have case studies showing that these aren't far-fetched ideas. It's not hard to find this information—even the government is in the game. Visit Business.gov for tips on greening a workplace. If the government is putting it out there, it's not too radical for your office. [122] [123]

> **Anticipate.** What will your employers ask? We know they'll ask how much it will cost to make a switch. We know they'll ask how you know it will be an improvement. They'll ask whether other employees will object. Gather all the facts to see it from their perspective and be prepared for their questions. [124]

> **Invest.** Step up and offer to take responsibility for the pilot program—whether that's making a [125]

run for supplies, creating signs, or educating your coworkers. Not only does this make it easy for the boss to say yes, but by investing in it, you're more likely to see follow-through. You lead by example and others will get invested, too. That is the kind of gumption that's worth showing at work—you impress your office while you improve it.

Of course, advocating to your bosses is only one method of liberalizing your work—but a liberal workplace isn't caused by convincing the execs of top-down changes. Like your neighborhood, your workplace is liberal because of how you engage with those who work with you.

**Engage.** You see these people at some of your most frustrated moments, in the doldrums of a routine day. You just want to keep your head down and keep to yourself.

If you do that, you'll never bring your progressive values into your workplace.

Don't go all Jonah on them right away. Building a connection is the first step in starting a conversation, which is a step toward creating a community, which is a step toward making change.

**Carpool.** If you are already planning to share the road, why not include your colleagues? Spend some time with coworkers outside cubicles and corporate culture. Learn to trust and rely on each other. Save on gas and get to use the carpool lanes.

**Make coffee for your coworkers.** Whether you make it at home and bring the thermos in to share, or you're the first to get the pot brewing in the office kitchen, create that shared resource. Get everyone invested in keeping the pot full. Save money and waste. Before you know it, people will be saying please and thank you and spending some time sipping and chatting together. If you start brewing coffee for others, they'll start brewing, too, and the pot will never go empty.

**Start a lunch co-op.** Could you coordinate your colleagues into an office potluck, giving you an opportunity to share and connect? If you don't make lunch, take turns buying or see who wants to eat with you when you get up from your desk. Part of living liberally is integrating your views and values into all the moments of your life—don't let work be an alienating, isolating exception. Take advantage of the social opportunity that lunch provides.

128

**Host work socials.** Whether your company organizes these or not, you can. If weekend plans seem a little too ambitious, start with an after-work happy hour. Coordinate birthday celebrations around the office. Let your coworkers see you in a different light. Don't just work together, play together.

129

**Spike the water cooler conversation.** People might not want to carpool or go out together, but in the course of the workday, they can't help but make small talk with you. Can you talk about more than who won *American Idol*? Could you talk about current events?

130

After you've engaged your coworkers a little, it's easier to talk politics. Don't lecture them as Jonah did, but draw them out. Find some common ground. If you diverge on a policy, learn the principles behind the policies you do agree on. If you conflict on a candidate, find out what topics matter most to your coworkers and speak to those issues.

131

The nice thing is that you know you'll see them again. When you knock on doors for a campaign, you have thirty seconds. When you start engaging coworkers, take your time—you'll see them tomorrow and tomorrow and tomorrow . . . and as long as you don't yell at them, they'll probably keep talking to you.

132 One last note on engagement: **make sure your coworkers are registered to vote.** Put forms on the front desk of the office, and offer to send them in. Don't be shy about asking every colleague if she or he is registered. Much like we accept recycling as a virtue, most people accept that voting is important. If you find someone unregistered or who moved and needs to re-register, you're doing him a favor.

Even if everyone is registered already, nobody will be annoyed that you're reaching out. Plus it's one more great way to start a conversation about politics.

133 **Organize.** You're becoming an advocate on your own and starting the road to engagement. Now, pull them together . . .

★ Your advocacy will be more effective if there are more of you . . .

★ Once you engage people, take them to a next step . . .

Now you're ready to . . . uh-oh, that scary word . . . organize!

We all know that President Barack Obama was a community organizer, a fact first celebrated by his supporters, then reviled by the right wing. All that really means is that he spoke to people who shared goals and met common obstacles. He helped them develop a strategy and work together. He helped empower them to move themselves forward.

Organizing in a workplace is much the same, whether your common goal is getting a new coffeepot or raising your wages.

You can circulate letters or petitions to get coworkers to sign on. You can enlist others to help you research solutions and propose alternatives to management. You can collaboratively imagine what would make your workplace a more comfortable environment and take the responsibility to make it happen.

That's all organizing is.

When you talk about organizing in a workplace, you may also be talking about labor unions, the collaborative force most responsible for improving working conditions, raising wages, distributing wealth, and creating a solid middle class over the past century.

Much of the organizing you do might have no connection to unions, and unions are by no means the only way to "work liberally." But they have been a great force in promoting progressive values in and beyond the workplace, and you can't talk about working liberally without talking about them.

The union movement in America grew out of the industrial era, as people crammed into cities to work in factories and realized they were being taken advantage of. By becoming a team, they were able to collectively negotiate for higher wages and better working conditions.

You might not be part of a union, but there's probably still reason you might want to thank them. A few of the accomplishments of organized labor:

★ weekends

★ paid holidays

★ minimum wage

★ child labor laws

Today, one out of eight Americans in our workforce is a member of a union—and new unions are forming all the time. However, not everyone will join a union—and creating a union at your workplace is not necessarily the best use of your time. That does not mean your organizing stops there, and it does not mean the labor movement means nothing to you, nor you to it. Unions know that their cause cannot be only about their members, and they fight beyond one contract at a time. Unions have been at the forefront of comprehensive immigration reform, expansion of health care, and the increase in the minimum wage . . . even though their members are documented American citizens, who often have employer-covered care and work for salaries above the minimum wage.

They are taking on battles that assume "we all are living for each other." Why do they engage these fights? To a certain extent, these are strategic. They don't want to have their own members and the good jobs they fought hard to create to get caught in a "race to the bottom" against plentiful low-paid work. On a larger level they recognize that they need to exist in a system where work is respected and working families can pay their way. They see that by fighting against underpaid work and undervalued workers in general, they help the larger cause.

That's why they've created ways for nonunion members to add their voices to the causes labor champions. Working America, a program of the AFL-CIO, is one example: a research and advocacy initiative that pushes for progress on issues that face all working families. It's a place where union and nonunion workers can fuse their interests and show that we're all in this together. You could join and bring coworkers with you—not because it impacts your own workplace, but because it's a way you can improve the workplaces of others.

You don't need a union card in order to start organizing in your own work life. You don't need to use tactics as confrontational as strikes and negotiations. Organizing is simply getting more people involved in the same agenda—and that involvement can lead to personal investment, which helps create a community of colleagues along the way.

Whether your fight is to get rid of the water cooler or get day care on-site, here are five ways you can start organizing today:

**Talk with your coworkers.** This is the simplest, but it's also the most essential step, which is why we keep returning to it. Share your concerns, and ask them what's on their mind. As you find where your interests overlap, you're naturally starting the process. All good organizing begins when people identify their own needs and goals for change.

136

**Delegate.** Remember all those steps to become an advocate? Researching solutions, anticipating concerns, stepping up to take responsibility . . . all of these are easier when you're not doing them alone. As soon as you identify areas where you and colleagues want to make change together, make sure everyone has a task. When everyone has a role, everyone has skin in the game. It's harder to back out, and more likely that everyone will lead and innovate in his or her own way.

137

**Circulate a petition.** Nothing like getting a good old-fashioned John Hancock down on paper to show you're serious about something. You can collect signatures from all coworkers, or have a letter-writing campaign in which everyone writes a letter on the same topic. Provide talking points or templates so the letters are on the same page. This is a basic, easy, and effective step toward organizing. It makes your ideas "real" to have people attach their names. As a practical matter, you could spend a lot of time explaining to each coworker, or explaining to management, what you're asking for. Have it written down, and it saves time. It feels more official. People take it more seriously.

138

139

And the petition doesn't need to be strident. You're not Thomas Jefferson listing the grievances against King George. It can be funny. Charming. Persuasive. Find the tone that fits you and your workplace. There's no reason your boss should feel defensive upon receiving these letters. The letters demonstrate there is an issue people are taking seriously enough that they took the time to put it in writing.

**Identify targets and allies.** In any setting—a workplace, a neighborhood, Congress—there is a constellation of different players who might be involved in your cause. Maybe they're naturally sympathetic, or they are the skeptics you have to convince. Maybe they're the ones who can give a green light, or just the ones who lob criticism but have no real authority. Take the time to map out who your potential allies are that you should recruit; who your real targets are that you need to convince; and who you might be able to ignore completely.

Don't waste time engaging the CEO if the office manager can make the change you want. Go to her directly. Or, if the topic does need the CEO's approval and relates to the work of the office manager, get her on your side first. Present the case and make her an ally—since the CEO will probably ask her opinion, and you don't want her to feel blindsided.

**Just do it.** Is there a change you could foster with your allies without requiring a green light? If so, make it happen. I think of the Green Guerillas, who took over abandoned lots and built community gardens. They never would have received permission, but once these flourishing green spaces existed, it was harder to take it away from them. Where is that opportunity in your workplace?

No, you can't change wages or vacation policy or flex time on your own. But you can improve the kitchen and environmental practices. You can start a feedback box or maybe even spruce up an area to make it a lounge. If you and your partners in crime can take initiative, it puts other people in the position of having to say no after the fact, which can be just as unlikely as them saying yes beforehand.

## Owning Liberally

Owning a business can make working liberally easier—you could just say yes to any of the ideas in the previous section; or can make it harder—you're now staring at the bottom line and caught in the 1,001 details of keeping a business afloat that get in the way of loftier goals.

Some would even argue that as a business owner, you shouldn't worry about being liberal; that your responsibility is straight-forward: to make money—and that's the only metric by which you should be measured. If you have investors or shareholders your responsibility is to them and to making them money . . . not to workers, unions, the environment, or any one of a number of external constituencies.

I first heard this argument when I was about twelve. At Passover one year, my one conservative uncle (a great guy who very will-ingly debated with the younger liberals in the family . . . also, by the 1990s, he was a Clinton voter, so "conservative" is a relative concept) and my father were debating business ethics.

My uncle asserted that you should treat employees well and be honest with them, as well as with investors and partners. Beyond that, business did not need to factor in "ethics." The mission of business was simply to make money.

My father had a different perspective. He had spent much of his life producing Off-Broadway theater, professional productions on a smaller, less expensive scale than Broadway.

He asked my uncle what he should do if he had a million dollars: produce one Broadway production or ten Off-Broadway productions? (The numbers would be much higher today . . . remember, this was 1990!) My uncle asked which had the greater chance of success; what makes a show successful; would the greater investment in one place guarantee a profit? I suspected, as a twelve-year-old, that investing big would make a show better known and give a greater chance of profits.

My father didn't argue which would or wouldn't make money. Instead he suggested asking fundamentally different questions.

If you invest in ten shows instead of one, how many more people do you employ? Ten times as many designers, directors, performers, stage managers—and because you're filling ten times as many theaters, you're also employing ten times as many box office managers, house managers, and janitors. You're putting more money into the hands of more working people who are now spending that money, and probably setting lower ticket prices that make it accessible for more audience members, who also eat at local restaurants and support that local economy. And you're making ten times the cultural offering to the world, able to bring a diversity of playwrights' voices, ideas, and issues into public discourse.

He could have made an economic argument about not putting all your eggs in one basket and diversifying investment to hedge bets. That didn't interest him. His work had dimensions other than profit. It was about the community—both the creative community and the community of professional workers—in which he was situated.

Working liberally, for an owner, is about understanding your business in a landscape that includes its workers, customers, and community.

Despite the stories we hear of corporate greed and indifference almost every day, there are still businesses that are trying to do right: to share the prosperity and opportunities that come with success. The businesses don't have to be behemoths like Google. Often it's the local stores that do best, because these shops know their community and care individually about their workers.

In Seattle, a greasy fast-food counter on Capital Hill shows that a business doesn't just have to go with the flow. Hourly servers often have the worst-paid and worst-respected kinds of jobs. At McDonald's, the servers are turned, as much as possible, into robots (read *Fast Food Nation* for more on that) and compensated poorly. Counter jobs are often the reason we need to fight so hard to raise the minimum wage.

144

Dick's, a fast-food joint in an orange hut that looks like a archetypal 1950s drive-through, does it differently. It has a sign in its window boasting of the benefits it offers employees. Dick's pays significantly higher than the minimum wage, offers health benefits and child care support to hourly employees, and compensates employees for time spent on their education.

145
146
147   148

They are not merely giving workers time off for education. They are not paying for professional development days that keep their workers in the corporate structure. They are paying for time workers spend improving themselves outside the work environment.

That's a sign of believing in investing in workers and cultivating loyalty that keeps them working there. Dick's prides itself on being a family business. Its employees become part of that family. Its website boasts sections on "community impact" and "giving." Its turnover rate is much lower than elsewhere across the fast-food industry.

Dick's burgers are greasy. They are not locally grown, grass-fed beef. This place isn't doing everything right. But when it comes to respecting labor, there's no question that Dick's has found a liberal way to be an employer.

Across the country, another business that takes working liberally in a different direction is Blue State Coffee. This company peddles Fair Trade coffee, opens its venue to community meetings, and supports positive environmental practices. Blue State does more to engage its customers and share their values: it donates a portion of its profits to local nonprofits.

Charitable giving by companies is nothing new. Blue State Coffee has added a fun twist. When you buy something, you're given a token—and you "vote" with that coin, dropping it into a container for one of several nonprofit recipients. Blue State makes its gifts based on what the customers vote for. Secondly, it's decided at each store to emphasize local causes. It is using this very routine act—buying coffee—to draw its customers, its neighborhood, its product, and profits into one ecosystem.

From the local burger joint to an internet giant, you can work liberally as a business owner. If you do it right, it's not a distraction from running your operation—the liberal approach should become an asset. It involves more people, engenders more goodwill, and returns rewards to the business. Here are five ideas where you can start:

**Respect work.** Compensate your employees well.

**Listen to your workers.** Ask for their ideas. Challenge them to improve the business.

**Share the wealth.** Limit your own compensation as you create ownership stakes for those who work for you.

**Know your community.** If you build relationships with your neighborhood, industry, and workers, it will pay back. Customers will pay more or will rally around you if you're in trouble. Your business is benefiting in many ways from community security, so you should be a partner in that.

**Have a longer—and larger—view.** Nothing creates greed as quickly as a short view. The best and most profitable businesses take a longer view. They share their success with their communities. These businesses affirm that we are all working for one another.

There are a growing number of networks to help business leaders share ideas for using their business to change the world. If you join Net Impact, for example, you find yourself part of a global organization that believes business can inspire positive change. Or consider the Social Venture Network if you want

154

155

156

157

to learn from other social and business entrepreneurs who believe that the common good and the bottom line don't need to be adversaries.

## Freelancing Liberally

There is another route besides being an employee or an employer that in some ways is the most liberal lifestyle of all: being a freelancer. Work from home, so there's no commute. Stroll to the coffee shop, where all the other freelancers (or, as they're sometimes called, "unemployed") have their Macs open, writing, designing, surfing the web. Make your own hours, wear whatever you want, take long vacations, and drink lots of organic coffee. Now that's the life.

Unfortunately, that's not really the life of most freelancers. Without a doubt, this scene is repeated again and again among underemployed twenty- and thirty-somethings in metropolitan areas, but most freelancers aren't quite so carefree.

I should note what I mean by freelancers. There's an insidious movement for major corporations to categorize more and more employees as "independent contractors"—this gets them around all sorts of rights and protections accorded to salaried payroll workers. So you have hotel chains that call the cleaning crews independent contractors and make them buy their own supplies . . . as though those crews have any control over their own hours or working conditions.

That's a sad, very un-liberal, and quite different story. I'm focused on people who may choose to work for themselves. They don't want to be in an office environment, they're trying to start up their own business, or their skill set is just more suited to a project-by-project basis. Not every freelancer wants to be independent, but there are many who are. Regardless of whether you're there by choice or by circumstance, there's plenty you can do to work liberally . . . and it doesn't require owning a Mac or camping out at a coffee shop.

First, there are the obvious environmental and cost savings:

★ Shorten, or eliminate, your commute. [158]

★ Eliminate office rent and utilities costs. [159]

★ Waste less paper, or at least have more opportunity to keep track of everything electronically. [160]

★ Limit investment in conference phones and additional lines (if you don't know about FreeConference.com, go there now!). [161]

★ Make your flexible time fit your family schedule. [162]

Those are all personal advantages (that come with the disadvantages of irregular paychecks, higher taxes, and more pressure to keep receipts). Can there be communal advantages as well? As a freelancer, where's your community? It's probably other freelancers.

You already see that in the coffee shops mentioned above: people feel camaraderie in those settings. Many freelancers find communal solutions for the services an office would normally provide: they often share printers, newspaper subscriptions, passes to research centers or websites, and bookkeeping services. Freelancers quickly realized that liberal truth: that freelancing together is better than freelancing alone. In several cases, they organized. [163]

**Coworking.** You may not want the overhead of an office, but it sure is nice to leave the confines of your apartment. Sometimes, the coffee shop doesn't cut it.

The coworking phenomenon is the arrangement of a shared space. It probably has a printer/fax /copier everyone can use. It has desks, but also flexible seating areas. It definitely has wi-fi. If it's worth its salt, it has coffee.

You don't simply come, take coffee, and leave. You pay by the month, week, or day for the ability to share these resources.

Costs are low; there's a collective spirit; everyone knows the rules and helps clean up, supervises, and provides security for one another. Many coworking spaces have added on cultural, social, and artistic elements: presentations at the end of the day; happy hours; transforming the office into galleries, hosting performances or parties at night.

This makes sense. The folks who share coffee and couches share culture; they are a community; and by having events there, they make it a home.

**The Freelancers Union.** Yes, you can laugh: it's sort of funny at first. Unions are for employees at huge companies. Freelancers are the opposite. But the Freelancers Union creates that delightful oxymoron with real reason: to tell those independent workers that they deserve the security and support of their peers in traditional labor and to create the collective mechanism to get it for them.

Artisan guilds for years helped set prices and guidelines for independent skilled workers, so it's not so absurd that such workers would join together. In modern America, it makes even more sense. Many workers have their health care, pension, and advocacy for workplace rights tied to their jobs. In this scenario, who speaks for the freelancer?

Founded in 2001, the Freelancers Union now represents more than 12,000 members, providing medical, dental, and other insurance at low costs. It's hard for an individual to get health care, and there's a reason that insurance companies pool risk. In the Freelancers Union, you pool your risk with your new community—you go into it together.

The Freelancers Union also advocates for the interests of their members in public policy discussions. In 2009, they scored a big victory when New York City eliminated the Unincorporated Business Tax for many freelancers. This had amounted to a double tax for many workers; now, many individuals will save up to $3,400 thanks to this collective effort. As labor unions fight for their constituents for better contracts and safeguards, this new union does the same for its members. You might work alone, but you're not alone.

## Volunteering Liberally

There's one other important way to work liberally—wherever you are in the labor chain. Living liberally means not living for yourself alone; working liberally means working for others as well. You have professional skills: now **volunteer** them.

166

Sure, there are volunteering opportunities to clean parks and paint schools. Are you a landscaper or a painter? No—you're an accountant, so volunteer to keep the books for a small nonprofit. You're a graphic designer, so make the posters for the community arts center. You're a nuclear physicist, so tutor kids in science.

Your work life should feed into this spirit of giving. It will make you feel better about your work in the end as well.

Yes, at the end of the day, you're tired of work—that's why they call it "work." But if you can work for the greater good—which you aren't always able to do in the course of your typical day—you'll be working liberally.

# CHAPTER 4
# PLAYING
# LIBERALLY

> *So keep fightin' for freedom and justice,*
> *beloveds, but don't you forget to have*
> *fun doin' it. Lord, let your laughter*
> *ring forth. Be outrageous, ridicule the*
> *fraidy-cats, rejoice in all the oddi-*
> *ties that freedom can produce. And*
> *when you get through kickin' ass and*
> *celebratin' the sheer joy of a good fight,*
> *be sure to tell those who come after*
> *how much fun it was.*
> — MOLLY IVINS

> *If I can't dance, I don't want to be*
> *part of your revolution.*
> — EMMA GOLDMAN

Liberals are somber, dour people who see the end of the world in every unseasonably hot day. They are judgmental fanatics who tsk-tsk your use of disposable plastic plates and reprimand you for not following the news. They are screechy activists who make your water-cooler talk uncomfortable.

Those stereotypes have haunted liberals and probably chase anyone active in politics, left or right. In fairness, there are a good number of humorless, overly earnest lefties and quite a few folks who think being a do-gooder means being a goody-two-shoes.

Those people may have liberal political beliefs, and their intentions may be in the right place . . . but they are not living liberally.

Being liberal isn't just about activism twenty-four hours a day. Nor is it only about working hard and making a difference through your labor. Living liberally requires that you connect to your community and celebrate the diversity, creativity, and joy you find there. It's working hard to ensure everyone has opportunities; but also making sure those opportunities include the chance to enjoy. In short, being liberal should also be about having fun.

The signers of our Declaration of Independence spoke of our inalienable rights: life, liberty—and here's the one we can sometimes forget—the pursuit of happiness.

Greed, self-interest, hoarding money, and wasting resources may be the conservative pursuit of happiness, but it's not the only way. We can pursue happiness in ways that respect the earth and our community and spread happiness to others.

## Socializing Liberally

167

Here's one idea to pursue happiness like a liberal: buy a pitcher of beer.

When you arrive at Rudy's and find Drinking Liberally, I promise you someone will offer you a beer before you even make it to the bartender. What inspires this generosity? It's in the spirit of the event to share, to welcome newcomers. And the bar also makes it easy—by serving pitchers.

Pitchers of beer—especially cheap pitchers (Rudy's, with $7 pitchers of Rudy's Blonde and $9 pitchers of our favorite, Rudy's Red, is incomprehensibly inexpensive for Manhattan)—embody the ideals of "drinking liberally." First of all, it just makes economic sense to buy by the pitcher. It's cheaper than buying four pints . . . and despite conservative rhetoric, liberals are good with making the most of our money.

Once you have a pitcher in hand, it's imperative that you share it. Before you know it, you've made three new friends. They're all delighted you just poured them a pint, and are eager to return the favor. You've created a welcoming environment that has pulled people immediately into your community. This generosity self-perpetuates: those three are very likely to order pitchers when they sense it's their "turn."

When your pitcher finally runs dry, some member of your community will refill it. You are all drawing from a shared resource, just like a well of drinking water in the center of town. If that well runs dry, everyone suffers, and similarly everyone is affected when your pitcher goes empty. So now you're not the only one looking after it—everyone is. More people invested in replenishing your resources, everyone with the shared purpose of making sure everyone is drinking.

Do you get the best beer when you order by the pitcher? Not necessarily. Do you get exactly what you want? Probably not. So if you want to forgo the communal experience, you can buy a beer of your choosing; you can purchase a bottle of a pricier, more refined, more exclusive brew. You'll have the gated community of beers—in a bottle, open to your lips and nobody else's. While everyone else is on the public transit of beer, you're whisking by in your Mercedes. Alone.

Which is fine if that's what you want to do. But nobody will care when your bottle is empty. And nobody will instinctively offer to pour you a refill. And when that cute girl walks into Drinking Liberally for the first time, you have nothing to offer her that says, "Welcome to our liberal community."

Drinking Liberally wasn't the first organization to realize that alcohol, in addition to being a social lubricant, is social glue. There's a long history of associations in America that use social bonds to foment a sense of identity and community.

There are the traditional "fraternal orders" like the Elks or Masons, membership-based societies with lodges and traditions. There is the Rotary Club, founded to bring together civic leaders to support efforts to promote peace, prosperity, and humanitarian causes. In a very different atmosphere, the union halls were a social/political space for many workingmen and working-women for many decades in the twentieth century. Traditional political clubs were social centers for their members.

So why did our idea seem so fresh and new if it's just a rehash of an idea that's been around for centuries? It seems that our generation never learned about these clubs . . . or maybe society had forgotten about them entirely. In _Bowling Alone,_ a book that inspired many of us, Robert Putnam explored this topic. As he documented, from the 1960s through the turn of the century, participation in "associations" declined precipitously— civic associations, parent-teacher associations, even bowling leagues . . . hence the title _Bowling Alone._

People weren't becoming Rotarians or Elks anymore. Union membership had declined. "Membership" had come to mean something very different over those decades. If you were liberal, you might be a member of the Sierra Club or National Organization of Women or People For the American Way, which meant you sent them a check every year and let their professional staff handle the advocacy. Nothing against professional advocates—we need them. However, it reduced the concept of "joining" to donating. You were rarely asked to do anything in person, so it was less likely you felt a connection to your fellow members.

Even if you were a "card-carrying member of the ACLU," you didn't go to movies about civil liberties together. The card, in some ways a badge of honor, was also a joke—it didn't create any shared experience with other cardholders beyond simply sharing a card.

Matt O'Neill and I, when we started our weekly club, had read *Bowling Alone* and viewed what we were doing as a response to the problems Putnam raised. We were reawakening a yearning felt by older liberals to reclaim that sense of fraternity. At the same time, we were offering it like a fresh course to younger liberals. However, by no means were we the only ones inspired to try to recreate social capital in America.

Scott Heiferman was a programmer and developer who had read Putnam as well. His solution: Meetup.com—a website that allowed people to self-organize around their particular interests. It wasn't a chat room or group blog where you could virtually meet others who wanted to practice French or share their love of Vonnegut or trade tips on raising pugs. It was a site that empowered people to arrange face-to-face gatherings. . . . to "meet up."

Meetups gained more national attention, especially in the political world, when supporters of Howard Dean in the summer of 2003 started using the platform to attract and engage allies. Dean Meetups were so successful that some people thought Meetup was created by Dean or was specific to politics (political clubs have never been their biggest gatherings). It is a coincidence, but no accident, that Dean Meetups and Drinking Liberally began at the same time. Concomitantly, people were organizing around concerts with "Music for America" and soon after there were jogging groups called "Run Against Bush." There was no vast left-wing conspiracy to create self-organized, localized, progressive events for each social preference. There was a shared desire . . . and suddenly tools that allowed us to realize our desires weren't so unique or absurd after all.

170 This spirit was not limited to anti-Bush energy in the summer of '03. Green Drinks was already thinking—and drinking—along the same lines, with monthly happy hours for people interested in the environment and sustainability.

Since the launch and success of Drinking Liberally, there have been copycat groups. Drinking Freely is a libertarian drinking club that openly cops to being a rip-off of our model. Not sure that they're taking off, but it's good to know that they are trying. Someone should tell them that libertarians are welcome to come to Drinking Liberally. Over a pint, we may find how much we have in common. Drinking Skeptically gives skeptics a chance to get together. We often get asked if there's an equivalent right-wing group. There isn't: Drinking Conservatively just doesn't sound like that much fun.

While drinking is a great social lubricant, it's of course not the only one. Food works as well. Eating Liberally is only one of a rich collection of groups that organize supper clubs, potlucks, picnics, and outings around healthy, local, and sustainable food practices.

171 One other such group is Slow Food USA. If you've never heard of Slow Food, think "fast food"—then think the opposite. As advocates, Slow Food is part of a movement to make us think about where our food comes from and our place in a larger food ecosystem. But I imagine foodies sometimes suffer the same stereotypes that liberals weather: that they're no fun. They want to take our sweets away and push us into an ascetic lifestyle.

Foodies would be shocked by that characterization as many quite deliberately make the case that their food tastes better than mass-produced, factory-farmed products of agribusiness. Slow Food's social network of local chapters combines their advocacy mission with the pleasure food can bring in a social setting to form bonds and build the overall movement.

Slow Food chapters talk about issues—and eat and drink along the way, whether through potlucks or outings to local establishments. They realized food politics wouldn't be as much fun if it were only politics . . . it needs the food as well.

We often say that Drinking Liberally is not the end point of political activism; we don't want people just to drink. We believe it's more likely that they'll make calls or knock on doors when friends invite them. In the bar, we build that community. We put newcomers and experienced activists into a position where they share a beer. We watch people walk down the slippery slope from a political conversation to a political conversion.

We're the gateway into liberal political activism. It's easy to have a drink. Then you meet someone who gets you to come to a meeting, and there someone convinces you to canvass. Before you know it, you're handing out fliers on a dark street corner in the icy rain on the first Tuesday in November.

We're not yet the Rotarians, helping fund worthy causes, or the Masons, with secret signs and lodges. We can dream. Someday, I hope people will wear their liberal identification as proudly as many have worn their union affiliations. I hope that in addition to taking action together, we'll also open our doors to each other. I know that if anyone identified themselves to me as a member of the Fraternal Order of Liberals, I'd give them a couch to crash on. I'd also buy them a beer.

# The Personal(s) is Political

## Finding a mate for your bleeding heart

**by guest contributor Katie Halper, Laughing Liberally**

What's a liberal girl gotta do to get a date around here? I mean, it's Valentine's Day and I don't have anyone with whom I can share my bleeding heart, exchange Fair Trade chocolates, recite the poems of Pablo Neruda, celebrate Valentine's Day, and, of course, more importantly, V-Day and Freedom to Marry day.

Sadly, you really can't judge a book—or zine or manifesto—by its cover. Someone who makes all the right moves politically can make all the wrong moves romantically, as I've learned from many a bad date. Having no luck in my search for Mr. Right, or Mr. Left, I decided to search online for liberal-friendly dating sites, in the hopes that by taking action, I could get some action. Well, here's what I found:

1. **Act For Love** stole my aforementioned pun and uses "Take Action. Get Action," as their motto. The site is basically a hipster wolf in an activist sheep's clothing. All it is, is a filtered version of the people who are already members of the online dating consortium shared by www.nerve.com, *The Onion*, *Time Out New York*, and the *Village Voice*. So if it's snarky love you're looking for, you may be in luck (and get lucky).

2. **Care2.com Singles** bills itself as a place to "find others who Care2 make a difference for good causes!" The

site is part of www.Care2.com, the environmentally oriented search engine, forum, and directory, with a shopping service that donates a portion of its sales to environmental and progressive causes. This site is not for the rabid horn-dog, because it bombards you with petitions before letting you get to their personals page. But I guess that's a good way to filter out the committed activists from the commitment-phobic wham-bam-thank-you-ma'am-ers. I don't know about the romance potential, but the site is great, so I joined anyway. Their motto should be Care2.com Singles: Come for the free online dating, stay for the free e-mail account, blog, photo sharing, and action alerts.

3.  There are tons of vegan and veggie dating sites for people looking to give or get a hot tofurky injection. **Veg Connect** describes itself as "Free Vegan and Vegetarian Personals—Make Rad Friends and Meet Awesome Singles." The site features PETA's "Don't Be a Milk Sucker" campaign—a cautionary tale that demonstrates how milk harms people, through Garbage Pail Kids–esque milk victims like Chubby Charlie, Lactose Intolerant Latoya, Ear Infection Enrique, Windy Wanda, and Pimply Patty. I also caught the surprisingly funny pro-animal, anti-veal, mafia spoof movie *Veal: Fughedaboutit*. So if you're a meat eater, or a milk sucker, you may want to "fughedabout" this site.

I would have liked to have ended this column with an encouraging "So what are you waiting for? Liberal love is only a username, password, and 'why you should get to know me' description away." But I guess my mother was right: a good liberal online dating site is hard to find.

For now, Let's just hope I'm not forced to "pull a Lieberman" (switch teams) and sign up on Republican Passions (even if it is an oxymoron), DatingRepublicans.com, or Hannidate (brought to you by the lovable Sean Hannity).

## Entertaining Liberally

Popular culture is called that for a reason: it's popular. Liberal culture doesn't need to stand in opposition to that. It may appear that politics and culture mostly meet in staid ways: slow, heavy-handed documentaries or exhibits on weighty themes. If that's the case, then it's a combination of culture and politics that brings out the worst in both.

When you connect the two you should experience all the joy of good entertainment, with the shared experience, creativity, diversity, and social consciousness of good politics. We know from *The Daily Show* and *The Colbert Report* that political humor doesn't have to be pedantic. If you know how to look, it isn't hard to find progressive cultural experiences that don't skimp on the entertainment factor.

### Comedy

Since I've mentioned Jon Stewart and Stephen Colbert, let's continue on this laugh track. They epitomize the power of using entertainment—and humor in particular—as a vehicle for real ideas. It's another one of those "gateway" moments: people who might never tune in to a show about politics will tune in to a show that makes them laugh. If the comedy can carry in it nuggets of truth—which is what good comedy has always done—then jokes play the role of the Trojan horse. The audience lets in the laughter, and discovers political messaging in its belly.

This is a terrific way to reach younger Americans. Studies have shown that for young Americans, *The Daily Show* is one of the major sources of news. Other studies have also concluded that people who consider *The Daily Show* their primary news source are significantly better informed than people who consider *The O'Reilly Factor* their primary news source. And young voters have been increasingly liberal in the last three election cycles.

Humor and liberal values go hand in hand. Talk radio, the domain of the right wing, often involves an authoritarian host who allows no room for shades of gray. He offers tirades that play off of fear, hate, and division, all of which are well suited for talk radio.

Liberal views tend to consider a larger context and are less black-and-white. They are more complicated, so tirades don't always suit them as well. They are less hateful, so require a more upbeat, joyful medium. These are characteristics of the best comedians, who subvert social settings, expose hypocrisy, overturn authority, and try to please, not frighten, their audience.

Have you seen conservative comedians? They're just not as funny. There are strong conservative strains through much of the comedy-club scene: misogyny, racial stereotypes, antigay rhetoric. It's ugly. It doesn't connect people. It's like a little boy who is so frightened that people won't like him that he becomes a bully and picks on the weaker kid in the schoolyard.

Sadly, that kind of comedy gets easy laughs. Furthermore, many comedy club owners want to play to a lowest common denominator. They worry that political humor will lose people, but everyone can join in a good fart joke or a rant about a woman being a "bitch."

The idea that comedy could be used to effectively promote progressive values inspired the creation of Laughing Liberally. Additionally, we wanted to give comedians the incentive to do more thoughtful comedy. Much as Drinking Liberally told people it wasn't taboo to talk politics in a bar, Laughing Liberally told comedians it wasn't taboo to talk politics in their set. Laughing Liberally sometimes plays to liberal audiences, where it serves the role of rallying and rousing the faithful. Other times, the comedians work to politically agnostic crowds, where the goal is to get the audience in for the comedy and make them leave with the politics.

Once again, this "new" idea wasn't so new. Nor are Stewart and Colbert the innovators behind this. One guy who has been doing it longer than any of us just got elected to the U.S. Senate from Minnesota. He was building off a longer history that has always seen the best comedians use their acts to speak truth to power . . . humorously. So check out some of these classics. They may turn your conservative uncle red in the face, or may just make him laugh himself to the left.

## A Few of America's National Comedy Treasures

**Mort Sahl.** At the Hungry I in San Francisco in the 1950s, "while other comedians joked about their wives, Mort joked about the president." He kept it up through his career, blazing a trail for others on this list. He was pointed without being too controversial, a Will Rogers manner with a smirk, red v-neck sweater, a *New York Times* rolled up under his arm, and a sharp jab. Lampooning the House committee that fueled the communist hunts, he quipped: "Every time the Russians throw an

American in jail, the Committee throws an American in jail to get even."

**Lenny Bruce** brought religion, race, and political ranting to the stage in an era that was shocked by it—the late 1950s. His use of the word "cocksucker" got him arrested for obscenity in the 1960s. A later charge resulted in an obscenity conviction that was only overturned in the late 1990s, thirty years after his death.

178

**Dick Gregory** in the 1960s was one of the first black comedians whom white audiences got to know—and he used that popularity to talk about civil rights through his material.

179

**George Carlin.** Famous for his routine that used the seven words you couldn't say on TV, his set made it all the way to the Supreme Court. He used his comedy to rebel, to critique, and to challenge convention.

180

**The Smothers Brothers** have made a half-century career of comedy—no small feat given that their antiwar leanings got their TV show canceled forty years ago.

181

**Richard Pryor** made a comedy career by discussing racism—yet despite profanity and provocation remained relevant enough that he won the Mark Twain Award for American Humor late in his career.

182

**Ellen DeGeneres** used her platform to challenge America when she and the character she portrayed came out on a mainstream national sitcom.

183

**Tina Fey** may have delivered the fatal blow to the McCain-Palin campaign as she delivered lines that will resonate longer than Palin's actual speeches and are destined to follow Palin into her doomed 2012 presidential bid.

184

## Movies

We all love the movies. They are delightfully escapist fantasies and can bring diverse views and ideas to the general public. *Guess Who's Coming to Dinner* featured a white family facing the fact that their daughter was bringing home her black fiancé. *Philadelphia*, with Tom Hanks, put the crisis of AIDS more firmly in the mind of mainstream America. Films can also have explicitly conservative themes, celebrating militarism as the later *Rambo* films did, demonizing "the other," and frequently portraying gays as sources of derision. These themes can be unintentional: take an example like the "comedy" *I Now Pronounce You Chuck and Larry,* which traded on gay stereotypes ostensibly to make a point about inclusion and tolerance.

Despite Hollywood's reputation as a liberal mecca and the left-leaning views of many actors and directors, most films work hard to be apolitical—avoiding tough issues, sticking with the mainstream, and pleasing the lowest common denominator. Even apolitical films, though, can be viewed through a progressive lens.

We highlight these ideas with Screening Liberally. In our film reviews, we don't just cover the latest Michael Moore creation or human rights film festivals. We also talk about whatever the mainstream is viewing with a liberal perspective. For example, we praised *Superbad* not just for its comedic qualities, but also for portraying male heroes who did not fall into chauvinist conventions.

Sure, when you go to a film you might want to support directors who reflect your values (Ron Howard shot an ad in which he dressed up as his old characters from *Andy Griffith* and *Happy Days* to discuss why they would support Barack Obama). Or you might skip films by those who don't (Mel Gibson's anti-Semitic, antigay tirades may sour you on his on-screen work). Or you might want to support certain companies; Participant Films, involved in An Inconvenient Truth and the feature Good Night, and Good Luck, has socially conscious cinema in its mission.

Separate from the political views of the actors, directors, and companies, here are things you can look for in the film to decide whether it's worth screening liberally:

**Portrayal of women.** Do female characters exhibit leadership, or are they always victims? Are they real characters with desires, or are they just objects in a game played by the men?

**Portrayal of people of color.** If the most prominent black character in a film is a large, sassy black woman, it might be time to ask what's with our society's obsession with that stereotyped body type. If the only two characters of color in a film pair up with each other, we might ask why it's so inconceivable for a white and black character to get together.

**Portrayal of gay and lesbian characters.** You realize you know a gay person in your life, right? If you don't think you do, then that's just more proof that not every gay person is a limp-wristed sex fiend—though so many of them in movies are.

**Deference to authority.** Many films—even fun, enjoyable ones— ultimately contain themes like "Know your place" or "Stick to your own kind" or "You should have listened to the authority figure all along." Not every film needs to have One Flew Over the Cuckoo's Nest levels of rebellion, but it is worth noting when the status quo is a little too celebrated or when the point of a film is that the character who rocked the boat really learned her lesson in the end. Even in a charming film like Forrest Gump with a known liberal star, Tom Hanks, these themes prevail. Jenny, after being involved in activism, is the lost soul. Forrest, who avoids challenging society, is the hero.

**Does it trade on love or on violence?** Sure, there is too much sappy sentimentality in many films . . . but ultimately, they often are supporting a world in which love is a driving force. It may be bad filmmaking, but it's not a bad theme. Films with wanton violence, though, send a different message. Michael Bay action flicks ask us to care more about explosions than emotions.

Before you go to the movies, check out reviews for these themes. Look at the posters or the coming attractions for signs of objectifying women or the next crass joke. When you see a film, share what you saw with others—let your friends see through your liberal lens.

In addition to the mainstream movies, there are other ways of downing a dose of feature films that truly reflect your politics. One way to screen liberally is to screen socially.

**Movie clubs.** Just as we have drinking clubs and comedy outings, there are plenty of groups organizing to see movies together. Some of them see socially conscious flicks, and others attend the latest new release in socially conscious company. These create the opportunities to share the experience, form bonds and friendships, and continue the conversation after the lights come up.

Putnam bemoaned bowling alone. Isn't viewing together better than viewing alone?

This interest spawned Screening Liberally, a network of film clubs. Chapters host independent documentaries to support emerging filmmakers around liberal themes, attend advance screenings of films that seek to reach a political audience, organize outings to wide-release films, and arrange group screenings at homes or other intimate settings of classics, or political features released to DVD or via download.

Plenty of local groups host these types of events, and you could find them at Meetup.com without too much trouble. One particularly impressive group is Brave New Films. BNF is a group that uses film as a medium to influence political discussions. It was founded by Robert Greenwald, a filmmaker who became well known for *OutFOXed*, which exposed explicit right-wing bias in Fox News. Since then Greenwald and BNF have produced features around labor practices and the Iraq war, then began to experiment with short videos that used the potential of the internet to go viral. They teamed up with different advocacy campaigns and helped create material more engaging than your typical e-blast or position paper—whether targeting the war in Afghanistan, the greed of finance tycoons, or the hypocrisy of television anchors.

They aren't just content producers, though; they are conveners as well. When they released *Iraq for Sale*, a film about the dangers of our reliance on military contractors, they bypassed the effort to be released in movie theaters and went directly to grassroots organizers. Brave New Films encouraged people to host house parties to show the film, gave them ideas for how to shape conversations and take follow-up actions, and made it very easy to use their website to organize and promote a screening. Thousands of events brought the film, and its ideas, across the country. [201]

While house parties are a great do-it-yourself approach, there is something about the big screen. If your progressive movie club wants a night out, consider choosing a cinema that will match your values: independent movie theaters. [202]

Most cities have these. Sometimes they are called the arthouse cinema, the indie movie theater, or even the second-run theater. If a film's message isn't mainstream enough to get the big money and wide distribution, this might be the place to find them. Just as frequently, though, these theaters do show wide releases—they may skip the latest torture-porn horror flick, but show the same quirky comedy or Oscar-bait drama as the larger houses.

Why support independent theaters? They are often the mom-and-pops. They have reason to be invested in a local community. They are more likely to host community events and support local nonprofits. They're more likely to think about how their business affects their neighbors. They're also more likely to show the independent films that might not get featured elsewhere. When you see even the wide releases at the small houses, you show the mom-and-pops that you appreciate their work and you keep them going!

Because of their personality, many of these theaters have already cast a liberal lens onto the films they're showing . . . so they will include *Superbad* . . . and probably pass on *I Now Pronounce You Chuck and Larry*.

You don't only have to rely on what the movie theaters are showing. If you want to see something at your local theater—something that might have more appeal than your living room can hold—you should go ahead and ask. Like any cause you want to promote, all you have to do is organize.

## Big Screen on Demand

203
a) **Research the film you want shown.** Find out if there is a distributor or if the filmmaker can give you the rights herself. Sometimes through the film's website you can learn if there are fees or restrictions associated with showing it publicly.

204
b) **Don't go it alone.** Ask friends if they'd commit to seeing the film if it came to town. Reach out to groups that might work

on the issues the film tackles and see if they would help host or promote a screening.

c) **Approach the local theater.** You're doing far more than submitting a suggestion to a box at this point; you're coming with information and with allies. Figure out who makes these decisions at the theater—owner, manager, curator. They're probably very interested in hearing what the community wants to see and would be delighted to know somebody wants to help.

205

---

There is a rich history of classic liberal films in America. Whether they think of themselves as liberal (*The Grapes of Wrath* about the Depression) or just happen to embody a liberal theme (*Footloose*—how can you not see political value in the rebellious city kid fighting for the right to dance in a puritanical town?), they deserve a second look.

206
207

Of course, there are so many, where to begin? Well, why not with the calendar? Below are a few selections that pair well with annual holidays. Watch them with your families and neighbors, or ask the local theater to host a screening series.

**Excerpted from "Progressive Films Throughout the Calendar Year" by Josh Bolotsky, Living Liberally**

**Martin Luther King Jr. Day**—Spike Lee's *4 Little Girls* provides a historical context to the 16th Street Church bombing in 1964, reminding us of the events

208

---

leading up to it and its legacy for the country. Rather than tsk-tsking those who either actively aided oppression or stood on the sidelines, Lee lets them dig their own graves, including a remarkable interview with former Governor George Wallace that one must see to believe.

**Valentine's Day**—For a film that breaks out of the heterosexist paradigm of most screen romances, check out *But I'm a Cheerleader*, the (beyond-camp) story of a budding lesbian romance. Two teenagers—one from the punk subculture, the other from a household of perfect grooming and cheerleader drills—are both sent to a "heterosexual reeducation" camp, where they find themselves rebelling with the other gay teenagers against the be-someone-else dogma, all while falling in crazy, exuberant teenage love.

**Presidents' Day**—*Dave,* a delightful what-if comedy about an impersonator of a George H. W. Bush–like president who gets to take the real president's place—and slowly but surely tweaks the administration to one that cares about people over profits. Kevin Kline is great as both the president and his look-alike, the film's protagonist. This hilarious film is one of the best early works of Gary Ross, who would later make the excellent, progressive parable *Pleasantville.*

**Earth Day**—*The Age of Stupid* is a chilling call to action, reminding us just how little time we have, and just how dire and potentially catastrophic the consequences are if we don't radically change course in response to climate change. Pete Postlethwaite plays a one of the few surviving humans in 2050, in a giant Noah's Ark–like archive of what's left of human civilization, tracing just how and why we didn't take the threat of climate change seriously enough, and waxing philosophical about just how it was that humanity consciously committed suicide. Beyond chilling—required viewing, watch it now.

**Memorial Day**—The best tribute we can pay our brave men and women in uniform is ensuring that we only ask them to make the ultimate sacrifice when there is no resort left. ***The Great Dictator***, one of Charlie Chaplin's best comedies (and certainly his best talkie), is a film made about one of those times. When supporting Hitler was not particularly controversial in public life, before Pearl Harbor and before the widespread knowledge of the horrors of Nazi Germany, Chaplin had the courage to make a film that not only directly parodies Hitler and fascism but also speaks eloquently of human brother- and sisterhood, and against bigotry in all forms, which includes a Jewish protagonist at a time where this was decidedly not the norm.

212

**Independence Day**—There are all sorts of great films made about physical courage in the service of patriotism, and all of them would be fine choices for the day: *Born On The Fourth of July, 1776, Saving Private Ryan.* Less recognized, however, are films made about civic courage, about those whose patriotism meant challenging the status quo to make America a better place, often at great personal risk. In that vein, I strongly recommend ***Good Night, and Good Luck***, a reminder of just how much risk to self it meant to publicly denounce McCarthyism. In the era of Glenn Beck and Sarah Palin conservatism, where Van Jones has to step down as Bush goes unprosecuted, it serves as a reminder that it requires courage to take on those who fight against democracy and in favor of public fear.

**Labor Day—*Norma Rae*** is one of those films that is now largely remembered solely as a source of Oscar montage clips—we see the picture of Sally Field with the scrawled UNION sign, and half-remember that this was from some important movie or another. Which is quite a shame, because *Norma Rae* is so much more than that. It's influenced just about every I'm-Taking-a-Courageous Stand, I-Am-Woman-Hear-Me-Roar film made since. As such, watching *Norma Rae* can be like watching a lot of seminal genre films—we can't help but think it's cheesy because we've seen this stuff so many times, until we realize that this film was there first.

**Halloween**—It's not a particularly original thought that horror tends to be the most innately political of genres—when it's all about finding the root of what scares us most, is there any quicker expressway to our politics? For a film that takes this observation and goes about as far with it as one can imagine, check out *The Last Supper,* a twisted mélange of black comedy, horror, and political satire that is truly sui generis in its originality, and not something you are likely to see replicated anytime soon. This is one of those films whose premise is so delicious that to even mention the main plot would be a little bit like blurting out the punchline before the setup is even finished. Let's leave it at this: The film is about a fear that every serious political thinker has at least once in his or her life: is political dialogue with those we disagree sometimes pointless? What about those fanatics with whom you can't reason? What if the simple fact is, that democracy can't deal with the fact that the world is simply better off without certain viewpoints being represented?

**Thanksgiving**—It's important for progressives to mention/remember that Thanksgiving can have a very different meaning for Native Americans. Chris Eyre's *Smoke Signals*, with a screenplay by Sherman Alexie, is one of the very few films ever made by Native Americans about Native American characters—and it happens to be a very funny family comedy that reminds us of how often these communities have been left out of the discussion entirely.

**Holiday Season (Christmas, Hanukkah, Kwanzaa, Winter Solstice, etc.)**—Can one even try to do better than *It's a Wonderful Life*? Where to even start? The protagonist fights to save his community in a time of widespread poverty, finds that wealthy entrenched power (as embodied by Mr. Potter) tries to undercut him at every turn, and realizes that wealth isn't as important as how much you help others in this life. A classic. (The fact that the FBI considered the film communist propaganda is worth noting.)

## Television

The big screen immediately offers more screening liberally potential than the small screen, but we shouldn't cut out a popular medium just because we don't like it as much. Sure, Robert Putnam points to television as a major factor in the decline of social capital, but there are plenty of ways of Tele-visioning Liberally.

There are occasions that will be broadcast over television that hold public interest, like people gathering in 1969 to follow the moon landing. This regularly happens with nonpolitical occasions: the Super Bowl and other sporting events or episodes of *The Sopranos* when people with HBO suddenly realized they were everyone's best friends.

Starting a few years ago, another community event started springing up once a year: the State of the Union. People were fed up with and scared of President Bush—but they felt like they had to watch. They had to know his next horrifying lie (yellowcake uranium) or newest out-of-the-blue distraction (manned travel to Mars). We felt a morbid duty to watch this speech.

We couldn't watch alone. Instinctively people started hosting watch parties—in their homes, in public spaces, even in bars. By Bush's second term, it was common for bars—which would have once said politics was bad for business—to tune into the address as patrons played a State of the Union Drinking Game.

It all comes back to booze.

Sip if he pronounces the word "nu-kyu-ler." Sip when he talks about "evil-doers." Chug if he invokes Jesus. Finish your drink if he adds a new country to the Axis of Evil.

This type of game proliferated from 2003 and 2008, and gave people an outlet other than screaming at the television. It gave them reason to share the night and led to people joining discussions and getting more involved in politics.

All thanks to the power of the television.

Election years provide countless opportunities for these gatherings. Every primary night and debate night became a cause to convene around televisions, like you were watching a sports tournament up to the championship game: election night parties, complete with winners and losers, game-time commentary, and chanting all across the country.

Not every year will have that same level of political television—but there are other opportunities to create these communal events. It might not parallel Barack Obama's acceptance speech, but it might still make good TV.

We all have televisions. . . . let's put them to work. Here are a few other ideas to make that omnipresent tube work for the greater good:

**Presidential press conferences.** When the president addresses the nation, he always does so in prime time. It's called "prime" for a reason. Watch it with your neighbors. You can answer each other's questions and share your reactions.

**Premium politics.** If you have HBO, you have a resource that you owe it to your friends to share. HBO produces and programs terrific documentaries that you might not otherwise see: *Baghdad ER*, about our military's emergency room doctors, or *Trouble the Water*, about Hurricane Katrina. In an era of watered-down news coverage, these films are some of the best journalism on television.

**Screening Liberally Oscar Night.** In addition to one-off events, there is some programming you can predict. Every year there will be an Oscar Night, and about 30 percent of your heart wants to watch. You want to see celebrities, you want to be in on the cultural moment, but you may not want to focus all of your attention on it. Watch it with others and make a game of it, just as people do with the State of the Union. Share some political movie trivia throughout the night. Compare notes on which nominated films had the most liberal themes. Guess at whose speeches will be the most radical. It's a night where you can invite the people who enjoy watching press conferences to come to something political . . . but also a little more popular.

**Share your favorite liberal shows.** Just as you're allowed to enjoy movies that aren't explicitly political, the same applies to TV. *The West Wing* was a liberal fantasy, especially since so much of it aired during the Bush years. Other shows—ones that promote diversity, include themes of subverting authority, or provoke debate in general—can be just as political without being as explicit. *Battlestar Galactica* got people debating torture and occupation. *The Wire* makes you ask questions about the drug war. Sitcoms can even be the source of good liberal values . . . how can we forget *Family Ties*? Pick your favorite weekly features and share them around.

Additionally, getting a group together is a great way to watch some of the best documentaries TV has to offer. PBS consistently runs compelling programming, including their series *P.O.V.,* and if you have HBO, you have access to some of the best documentary work being produced. These are programs that will get you talking and sharing, and they are good opportunities to cultivate your local political community.

**State of the Union.** We might not groan, grimace, and giggle as much without W. to kick around, but the president's annual address to the joint session of Congress is still a must-watch. Even with someone articulate behind the podium, it doesn't hurt to have a drink in hand.

**Big Picture for the Small Screen:** You know that *The Daily Show* and *The Colbert Report* will do a better job delivering you the day's events than most news stations, and Keith Olbermann and Rachel Maddow have brought the right's feisty fight to the left, with charm, smarts, and good ratings. But when you decide to queue up Netflix and delve back into TV land, here are a few suggestions from our Liberal TV Guide:

*All in the Family*. Archie Bunker was a typical American guy in a world run wild: a white, middle-class father, he had to confront civil rights, student unrest, and a constantly changing society. The creation of Norman Lear (who later founded People For the American Way to battle the impact of the religious right), this show gave us the lovable curmudgeon who kept learning new lessons about our new America and brought us all along with him.

*Murphy Brown*. Any sitcom that picked a fight with a sitting vice president must have done something well. Dan

Quayle's criticisms of Murphy's single-mom status seem almost quaint now. At the time, it reminded us that TV characters could have articulate (and entertaining) arguments on-screen. It also provided the fantasy of reporters who really pursued the story, with little regard to the network's bottom line.

**The West Wing.** You would watch how Jed Bartlett's moments of indecision inevitably end with him returning, more forcefully than ever, to a passionate, committed, bold agenda. And you would wish that this show's writers were advising the Clinton White House, and not vice versa (or were now advising Team Obama). Infectious dialogue and engaging characters get to play on a stage of global importance . . . and in the end, more often than not, create an America that would make us proud.

**Maude.** Another Norman Lear creation, this show featured Bea Arthur (later of *Golden Girls* glory) as a liberated woman—outspoken, opinionated, and not afraid to bring up issues to those around her . . . and those watching at home. Famously, a number of episodes dealt with Maude having an abortion, bringing a level of honesty to the discussion that is rarely seen in the more cautious accidental-baby tales of today like *Knocked Up* and *Juno*.

**Family Ties.** Someday, I hope some young Republican explains to me why they love Alex P. Keaton, Michael J. Fox's breakout character, a young conservative who kept learning liberal lessons by each episode's end. Not that liberals were wholly loved—his ex-hippie parents were teased for being too flighty and far-out—but overall it was a show that talked about equal rights, elitism, wealth disparity, and electoral politics.

***The Simpsons.*** One episode brings us to "Springfield Republican Headquarters," an underground lair populated by a rogue's gallery of villains: corporate (Monty Burns), oil (the Texan), and just creepy (Dracula). No party or politician is spared lampooning, but generally we get to follow Homer as his accidentally right-wing antics, like heading up a local militia, lead him into trouble. Thankfully, the sensibilities of more communal-minded characters with progressive perspectives, like Homer's daughter Lisa, save the day.

238

***Saturday Night Live.*** Before there was *The Daily Show* and *The Colbert Report,* Dan Ackroyd was Richard Nixon and Chevy Chase took falls as Gerald Ford. The dead-on satire of the Clarence Thomas hearings, the 1992 Democratic debate where candidates competed to not lose to George Bush, and the Bush-Gore debates of 2000, which gave us "strategery," will live on as vividly as the real events they mocked.

239

***Sesame Street.*** Teaching kids to read and count is one thing; teaching them to do it in Spanish is a little radical. Everything about *Sesame Street*'s early years was a little radical: it gave us an interracial and inter-human–Muppet vision of city life, taught us to embrace differences, to be kind to each other, to accept all sorts of lifestyles, and to love one another: whether you're green, blue, yellow, feathered, or furry.

240

## Arts Collectives/Theater

TV and movies have mass appeal because they use mass media. We'd be foolish not to support liberal lessons in such a widespread form. There is also, though, something special and remarkable about the experience of live performance. You feel that thrill of seeing the actors right in front of you, and you know they feel the energy off the audience, hear the laughter, applause, and gasps. Audience and performer are more genuinely connected in live theater, allowing at times for greater sincerity and emotional pull. It also creates a bond: you are not only sharing the experience with other theatergoers, you're sharing it with those onstage. There is a reason why rock concerts can transport people, why live comedy can bring you to uncontrollable fits of laughter, and theater can move and shock and engage you. That genuineness stays with you longer, in many cases, because it feels more immediate.

Theater also has a long history of carrying social messages: whether through satire or allegory, from the Greeks through the labor playwrights of the Depression, upending the social order in Shakespeare or offering a look into a world upended as theater discussed gender, race, and AIDS with greater honesty at the end of the twentieth century.

Unfortunately, many people view theater as a rarefied experience—and that's often a justifiable impression. Theater is usually more expensive than a movie; that's just the economy of live performance.

Fortunately there are alternatives that make theater, and other live performances, accessible. Art collectives around the country rely on volunteer energy, artists who are ready to take risks, and maybe some nonprofit funding to showcase performances you might not see elsewhere. Moreover, these venues sometimes compete financially with a night at the movies.

In New York, Living Liberally has had a sibling in the nonprofit venue <u>The Tank</u>, an organization I helped start in 2003. The Tank is a home for performances and public affairs across disciplines: theater, film, comedy, music, dance, mixed media, puppetry, reading, speakers, forums, debates, meetings, and parties. Ticket prices are capped, so that taking a risk at The Tank feels as affordable as taking a risk at the AMC. Performers aren't paid, but they aren't charged, either. The door is shared between the venue to cover costs and the performers to recoup their expenses. It's a setup where nobody gets rich, but nobody— including the audience—goes broke.

The goal of this financial structure is to serve as a place that prizes creativity, collaboration, and experimentation over commercialism. More than four hundred shows a year take place at The Tank, serving more than a thousand artists and tens of thousands of audience members. It's more than just a home for the arts; it strives to be a center of free expression and community involvement. It strives to be a democratic space.

This type of cultural offering should not be seen as the unique possession of a big city. Though they take different forms, this same spirit—and sometimes the same model—exists around the country.

Look to Iowa, the state in which Kevin Costner once said, "If you build it, they will come." Zach Manheimmer, a transplant from the off-off-Broadway theater world, must have seen *Field of Dreams* too often, because he took that advice. With the help of local partners, activists, funders, and loads of volunteers, he took over a sprawling office space—which had been home to both Obama and Dean's presidential campaigns in the Hawkeye State—and started the <u>Des Moines Social Club</u>.

What is it? You could call it a theater. It has plays. It also has circus classes, poetry slams, and music. So maybe it's a performance venue. Then how do you explain the lounge where cheap local brews are poured, informal organizing meetings are held, and a small stage in the corner tantalizingly suggests an open floor—a Speaker's Box with amplification? There's also the gallery. So it's an art house . . . or a creative playground. It also has meeting rooms for conference and community gatherings, and soon will have classroom space. You could call it a community center . . . but it feels too cool.

There's a reason they called it a "social club"—they had visions of some public space that shared all these attributes. They felt the need to create a space that housed all manner of arts, but not only arts. They wanted a venue that encouraged a liberal sensibility, but wasn't explicitly political. They wanted to make everyone who walked in the door not only feel that they wanted to come back but also believe they were one of the owners, in some way responsible for coming back to contribute to the community.

In the heart of Iowa.

There are different models of how volunteers take ownership over creating a cultural experience for a larger community. It may not be Broadway, but it's more affordable and open, more involved and interactive, and in all of these ways, it's liberal.

## A First Act on Liberal Theater

Nothing wrong with an old-fashioned play, if you can afford to go. Whether you catch it at your community theater or make it to a professional house, there are great works of drama that fill out your liberal arts education. Bertolt Brecht, the German playwright, once said he didn't want to create a play that angered or inspired audiences just long enough for them to make it to their car outside the theater, then forget about it on their drive home. Here are a few plays you don't forget about—and inspire us to Live Liberally.

**_Lysistrata._** Originally performed in 411 B.C.E., Aristophanes' comedy tells of efforts of the women of Greece to end war by withholding sex from the men until the war is over. 243

**_Inherit the Wind._** Based on the Scopes Monkey Trial, it recounts a small town putting evolution on trial—and with it, free-thinking, intellectual curiosity, and science. 244

**_Mother Courage and Her Children._** Bertolt Brecht creates a story of a woman who seeks to profit from a devastating war but only meets further devastation. 245

**_The Cradle Will Rock._** A 1937 musical by Mark Blitzstein, it was set to be directed by Orson Welles and produced by John Houseman. The political nature of it—and possibly pro-communist themes—got it closed down. The production company famously rented another theater and did a reading of it. As famous for its context as for its content, it is a reminder that some people find theater so powerful they seek to stop it. 246

**_Waiting for Lefty._** Clifford Odets is one of the playwrights most associated with the WPA era, and this is one of his most famous works, which actually led to audiences shouting "strike" in solidarity with the characters in the play. 247

**248** *Twelve Angry Men.* Inside the jury room, as jurors' personal prejudices shape their willingness to convict, one skeptical juror stands to make his case.

**249** *Master Harold and the Boys.* Athol Fugard brought the reality of apartheid South Africa to the American stage with this beautiful play about how racism and segregation infect everyone in society.

**250** *Hair.* Let the sun shine in! *Hair* caused a stir as it depicted the hippie counterculture of the late 1960s, introduced a slew of new American slang and profanity to the American stage, and ended act 1 with a fully nude cast. The antiwar message resonates over the years, as does the embrace of freedom and peace and questions about how characters should live and love in today's world.

**251** *Les Misérables.* The setting is one where the poor are wrongly imprisoned, persecuted, and oppressed. The protagonists, however naively, try to make the system right.

**252** *Rent.* Written at a time when contracting AIDS was a death warrant, this musical features characters who sing about life—about making every moment count. And in "La Vie Bohème," lyrics praise Maya Angelou, Václav Havel, and antipretension iconoclasm. Try to make all that rhyme.

## Music

Theater has had to fight to feel little-d democratic at times. Music, though, has always been a populist force. Maybe it's because you don't need sets and lights, you can just pick up an instrument, and so more ragtag bands find a way to be heard. Maybe it's because there is something raw and emotional that accompanies music, or because for so many teens music is a countercultural escape.

You can find the independent venues near you or find the playlist that speaks to you online. Here are a few suggestions for to add to your **Soundtrack for a Liberal America.** This mix was assembled by activist, technologist, and music-lover Franz Hartl with additional contributions from other allies who want you to Rock Liberally.

**Public Enemy** — *Fear of a Black Planet.* Chuck D is the godfather of revolutionary music, and this album is as sonically dense and aggressive as any album released since.

253

**Black Star** — *Black Star.* Before he went to Hollywood, Mos Def highlighted a new political consciousness in hip-hop. Talib Kweli is *THE* dominant political rapper today. Together, they made an album that set the stage for a lot of what Brooklyn is about today.

254

**Le Tigre** — *From The Desk of Mr. Lady EP.* While some will say that Kathleen Hanna's best work was with riot grrrl pioneers Bikini Kill, there's no beating her later band Le Tigre for danceable left-wing politics. "Get off the internet! Destroy the right wing!" Yes.

255

**OutKast** — *Stankonia.* "Bombs over Baghdad" is an eerily accurate political description of 2010, even though it came out in 2000.

256

**Radiohead** — *Kid A.* Arguably the most significant band of the past twenty years. The album showed you how dark and cold things were going to become without being bleak. But letting you know, at the same time, we are going to win (eventually).

257

**The Clash —** *London Calling*. When punk kids said they got their news from The Clash, this is what they were talking about.

**Discount —** *Love, Billy*. Allison Mosshart's pop-punk anthems are so sweetly melodic that you can easily lose sight of her politically astute lyrics. Get this for the cover of "Waiting For the Great Leap Forward" alone—then get all their other stuff for good measure.

**Marvin Gaye —** *What's Going On*. Can we be sexy and political? Yes, we can.

**Fela Kuti —** *Expensive Shit*. People need to KNOW the Fela Kuti story. Required learning, no exceptions.

**TV on the Radio —** *Return to Cookie Mountain*. So we had the Iraq war and Katrina, we were fighting back, and the dialect created by fighting back was making us into something new. This is the sonic interpretation of what the post-9/11 decade felt like.

**Dar Williams —** *Mortal City*. To be listened to right before debating a right-wing uncle on Thanksgiving, especially the wonderful track "The Christians & the Pagans." Her songs are punchy stories, brimming with insight, wit, and empathy.

**Rage Against the Machine —** *Evil Empire*. Politically uncompromising and aggressive.

**Bruce Springsteen —** *The Ghost of Tom Joad*. A reminder of what we are fighting to preserve.

**Ani DiFranco —** *Up Up Up Up Up Up*. The first track, "'Tis of Thee," is for when the battle seems unwinnable and you need to keep on going regardless.

> ### What if you were Playing Conservatively?
>
> You'd yell that the referees are biased against you, when in fact you appoint them and pay them. You'd guffaw and applaud at a comedian who cracks a really great joke about how his cabdriver spoke with an accent. You'd be part of an all-white country club.

## Traveling Liberally

When you're ready to break away from the everyday and find new playing fields, it is time for your liberal getaway.

You could venture into the wilds of our "big government" national parks. You could take a road trip to great historical sites from the [267] civil rights or suffrage movements. You could vacation to a place where you volunteer building homes part of the time with an [268] organization like Habitat for Humanity. You could find tips for environmentally friendly hiking (carry out what you carry in; [269] respect paths so you will not harm wildlife); or socially conscious [270] hunting (walk to the hunting grounds rather than driving in). You could join Karma Krew, a group that combines yoga with [271] community service. You could tour minor league ballparks to [272] get your fill of sports while supporting smaller markets, local businesses, and less-corporate teams. Or you can just go to the beach . . . and not feel guilty. It's your vacation! You don't have to work or learn every moment. But wherever you go, there are a few things you can do:

**Find the local diner.** There can be an instinct to go with what you [273] know: Look, a McDonald's! A Starbucks! An Applebee's! You'll have a much richer experience, though, when you go local. You support the local economy in a more meaningful way, spending at places with roots in the community. You're also more likely to get an authentic view of the area. You can ask for stories about where you're visiting, hear the political views of the waitstaff or other patrons, and learn about local happenings you might not have known about. And, in the end, the food will be better than at Applebee's.

**Read the local paper.** You're on vacation to avoid reading, I know, but pick up the local paper—whether it's a one-paper town, or a mid-sized city with free alternative weekly. This is where you'll learn what's going on. I'm not saying you need to become an activist in your four days someplace, but it's nice to know what the local folks are talking about. Once you have some grounding, ask them about it. Strike up a conversation. They'll be pleasantly surprised you know anything about their area at all, and usually they're more than eager to share.

**Reuse and recycle.** Vacations offer easy opportunities to drop all your good habits . . . and maybe that's part of why you go on vacation. That said, don't take a break from recycling. Hotels don't always make it easy to do—so ask them. Ask whether trash gets sorted or if there's a way for you to sort. Look around for recycling on the street if your hotel doesn't offer it. It may take a little work, but it'll make you feel better. And by asking, maybe it will put pressure on the hotel to make it easier for their guests. Hotels can change their behavior. Somewhere along the way hotels realized they shouldn't launder towels every day. It was probably a cost-saving measure disguised as environmental awareness, but why shouldn't we tie those two goals together?

**CouchSurf.** Want to save money, meet some like-minded, inclusive folks, and participate in a great collectivist social experiment?

People have always crashed on the couches of friends and friends-of-friends. Now you can do it by becoming part of a community of CouchSurfers who offer their beds to others and ask for that same courtesy in return. Rather than word of mouth, there are websites like CouchSurfing.org that make it easy to do. You're not swapping per se—rather you're entering a large market of people who are willing to trust and open their homes to one another.

Would you rather just stay in a hotel, not have to talk to strangers, have a guaranteed experience? Sometimes, yes. Other times, you end up in a new town, and it would sure be helpful to have someone who knows the area, the sites, the transit, the night-life . . . and someone who, because they're a CouchSurfer too, probably gets where you're coming from.

**Tip well.** Every country and culture has a different approach to tipping. But don't be fooled: if Europeans don't tip waitstaff, it's because their servers are paid well. Ours are not. Nor are our cleaning crews, doormen, porters, drivers . . . and their employers justify their low pay by arguing that they should factor in tips. So support the local economy and show your love of labor by respecting their work. Plus there are enough insults hurled about tourists; do your part to buck that trend.

277

**Wear sunscreen.** Skin cancer's no good. And public health threats ultimately cost us all. Be smarter than that.

278

## Imagination Gone Wild

A section on Playing Liberally isn't complete with a few examples of simply absurd playfulness. In 2003, the flash mob was popularized. A store clerk would look up to see that 150 people had just crowded into her store, and one minute later they were all gone. In a park, fifty people would simultaneously pull out

279

their phones and shout "Sell, sell, sell." These absurd acts of coordination were a mix of street theater, public prank, and well-organized group dynamic. People would receive an e-mail or text message with odd directions, and they would do what they were told. Why? Because it was fun.

Is it liberal? People who never met before were working in concert. They were creating a public experience that they and innocent onlookers shared. They made people think about public space in a different light. They were leaving a residue of trust and joy . . . people came away smiling at strangers, feeling like there was value in engaging the outside world. So, yes, it's liberal.

280   One particular group that has used this method well is Improv Everywhere, which has executed a series of stunts, most notably the No Pants Subway Ride. People receive instructions to board a certain car of a certain train . . . wearing no pants. Eventually the other riders start to notice that not just one or two people are pantless, but dozens. At first it's odd, or alarming. Then it's amusing. As more people get on at each stop, it's downright entertaining, even astounding, and people find themselves laughing together on a subway car. Finally, a man enters the subway with a stack of clothes: "Pants for sale," he shouts, and everyone bursts into hysterics.

Why not? Why not draw people into a surprising comedy and make them feel a connection they didn't know was there?

281   What would happen if this energy was turned to politics? One street activist group that did just that was the Billionaires for Bush, a satiric guerrilla group that would counterprotest liberal demonstrations with signs promoting greed and oligarchy. In 2004, they built a community around protesting and having fun. On tax day, they staged rallies at the post office, "thanking"

regular people for paying taxes so "billionaires" wouldn't have to. During the Republican Convention, when protestors were denied a permit to rally in Central Park, the Billionaires set up a game of croquet and thanked the city for keeping the rabble out of "their" park. Billionaire teams popped up around the country—with guidance and inspiration from the originators, but with the charge to make their own mischief locally. People had the chance to play dress up and get media coverage that contributed to political discourse. (In the health care debate, they turned into Billionaires for Wealthcare, showing up at the "Tea Party" rallies with slogans like "Let them eat Advil" and "Cigna / Palin 2012.")

Shortly after the 2008 election, New Yorkers found themselves being handed free issues of the *New York Times* as they entered subway stations. What they hadn't realized was that the paper was for a date in the future. They soon saw, though, that the paper was from an alternate reality: one where the Iraq war had ended, the Bush team was being prosecuted for their crimes, luxury taxes were imposed on the wealthy, and subsidies were going to green jobs and farmers' markets.

It was a taste of what the world could look like, a prank of possibility. And it was pulled off by some established pranksters, working with advocacy groups, and getting hundreds of volunteers to distribute the papers throughout the city.

You saw people on the subway smile and laugh; some looked concerned, while others looked hopeful. It earned media coverage, which only helped the stories travel more widely and sent people to the online version—an exact replica of www.NYTimes.com with a host of phony, and quite inspirational, stories.

The creators were pranksters and politicos. . . . and they were playing liberally.

# CHAPTER 5
# LEARNING LIBERALLY

> As Mankind becomes more liberal,
> they will be more apt to allow that
> all those who conduct themselves as
> worthy members of the community
> are equally entitled to the protections
> of civil government. I hope ever to see
> America among the foremost
> nations of justice and liberality.
> —GEORGE WASHINGTON

These pages provide some playful ideas for liberalizing your life, and there are plenty of other guides to going green, making a difference, saving and sustaining, making friends, and influencing people. Let me be honest: any how-to book can only urge you along a bit. It can open your eyes, suggest a few steps, but rarely will it transform you.

Your worldview and your daily lifestyle are shaped by more than a quick read. They are the results of a host of influences, some which have been lifelong, and some which bombard you every day. How you were raised, whom you speak with and listen to on a daily basis, where you turn for news or inspiration or to discover how to solve a problem—these are the influences that more deeply shape your engagement with the world.

You can't do much about how you were raised, but you can think seriously about how you'll raise others. You can make choices about where you go for information and insights, and think about when and how to challenge the status quo. In this way, day in and day out, you will be living liberally as a result of learning liberally.

Before we get into what you can try out on your own each day, let's tackle some big issues: without question, we're raised with certain conservative biases. I don't mean that you need to get out from under the shadow of a religious-zealot mom or Reagan-loving dad. I mean that our society—our schooling, our cultural inheritance, the habits we pick up before we know any better—contains significant right-wing lessons.

## Conservative Falsehoods We Need to Unlearn

★ **America is a nation of rugged individuals.** In fact, our greatest successes have always been collective in spirit or action.

★ **In America, you pull yourself up by your boot-straps.** Actually, we see how education and opportunity are often either passed down as legacies of the wealthy or are provided to all by the efforts of the state.

★ **"In God we trust,"** as emblazoned on our currency. America's origins and proudest moments have often been when we have allowed people to keep their religious beliefs as private choices, out of the public sphere.

There are also some terrific liberal messages we're raised with as gospel, whether they are true or not. Conservative messages are often proven a lie by the realities of how America works; but our liberal ideals have often fallen short through our history of segregation, disenfranchisement, wealth disparity, and militarism.

## Liberal Ideals We Want to Believe

★ **"All men are created equal,"** and America is on a march to greater and greater enfranchisement and rights.

★ **We have a country of laws, not of men,** and even our highest law can be amended because laws need to reflect a changing country.

★ **"Life, liberty and the pursuit of happiness,"** "e pluribus unum," and "truth, justice and the American way," are our shared language suggesting a nation of common fortunes, mutual respect, and tremendous tolerance.

America is often not as good as our principles. We are, however, far better than our more conservative myths. So there is really a double mission in learning liberally:

**1)** discredit and dismiss the conservative tropes and

**2)** honestly assess where we fall short of the liberal values.

Criticizing our country isn't "anti-American"—from the beginning, our founders were often outspoken about their concerns for the direction of the nation, and every great change—abolition, women's suffrage—grew out of people offering thoughtful critiques of our country.

Even if your goal is to emphasize the liberal legacy of our great nation, it doesn't hurt that cause to point out where we're lacking. Hold up those liberal themes as the ideal. Then the story of how America improves is part of the liberal lesson about our country.

It would be a separate project to catalog and disassemble the conservative lies that have snuck into our national consciousness. It would be an additional separate project to tell the story of America through the liberal lens, and where we still have further to go to reach the rhetoric of our nation. We're not going to do it all right here, but let's start by looking at what we've "learned" and maybe by unlearning a bit.

Growing up, I—like so many public elementary school kids—said the Pledge of Allegiance. The Pledge could be viewed as a great liberalizing force that creates a shared experience for all schoolchildren and asserts they are all part of a greater society; or it could be an authoritarian tool to brainwash us into submission. The fact is, it often becomes an act of repetition. Kids race to say it as quickly as they can. Most mumble through without thinking about the meaning, and many might not be speaking the correct words at all.

One of the few times as a child I was forced to stop and think about the Pledge was when a substitute teacher taught our third grade class. Mrs. Ginsburg was a regular substitute, and many of us had known her since first grade. When she led the Pledge that day, though, we noticed that she skipped a few words.

"And to the republic for which it stands, one nation," she intoned, then paused. Then continued, "indivisible, with liberty . . ."

She'd forgotten to say "under God," and we noticed. But we figured: she's old—chuckle and let it pass.

However, after the Pledge, she pushed us. "Did anyone notice what I did differently?" Nobody wanted to speak up and embarrass her with the fact she'd forgotten the words. "Did anyone notice what I didn't say?"

Finally, one student piped up. We all felt a little sorry for her that she'd flubbed it, and were confused why she was making such a big deal. She, though, wasn't embarrassed at all. "We have a separation of church and state in this country. You can practice whatever religion you want, or no religion, and the country protects your right to do so. But that also means you shouldn't have to say 'under God' when you pledge allegiance to your country."

That day wasn't a game-changer for any of us. We laughed it off, and wondered why we were spending so much time on it. It has, however, stayed with me. Over the years, as I learned more about our country, and the church-state separation, as I came into a political consciousness that was more concerned with those issues, I remembered what Mrs. Ginsburg hadn't said . . . and was thankful to her.

Mrs. Ginsburg wasn't being a radical. In some ways, she was the more traditional one. The words "under God" were added to the Pledge under the Eisenhower administration, as we strove to distinguish ourselves from the "godless communists." It's not that long a tradition, and you could argue—as some have tried, all the way to the Supreme Court—that it has no place in the public expression of belief in our country.

I tend to take a live-and-let-live approach. If you believe that God is watching over us and joining our journey, then say "under God." If you don't, or don't think it's appropriate, skip it. Hopefully, someone will hear that pause in your oath and ask you why, and maybe you'll plant a seed that will undo their formal education down the road. If it makes your Pledge more intentional, and you truly consider what you're saying and why, that itself is a liberal step forward.

Restoring an agnostic Pledge isn't the most important battle in pulling our education to the left. It's more an example of how one person can help you scrutinize the world in a new way, how she can encourage you to think outside the box and ask non-obvious questions. That's a key ingredient to learning liberally.

With that spirit in mind, and with the honest acknowledgment that we're not going to tackle our entire upbringing in this chapter, here are a few places to start in your reimagining of America.

### Our liberal history: Ten great moments and why they make us proud liberal Americans.

**The Declaration of Independence.** There was more than one reason the American colonies sought separation from the British, and they ranged from what we might consider the left (more representation) to what we might call the right (antitax). When the project of drafting this Declaration was handed to a young Thomas Jefferson, America was set on a liberal course. Asserting that "all men are created equal," suggesting a society based on commitment to one another and not loyalty to a crown, and assuming that participatory, representative democracy was a greater form of governance, T. J. laid out a fundamental set of liberal values that our country has been working to live up to ever since.

**The Revolution of 1800.** In America's earliest days, there were some who imagined a president would be as enshrined as royalty. George Washington's decision to only stand for two terms confounded that expectation, and quickly political parties emerged as a new test for the cohesion of our young democracy.

John Adams won the election in 1796; then in 1800, when Jefferson beat him, we faced a new unknown: how a transfer of power across parties would work in our country. Despite the high rhetoric and deep passions of some of Adams's supporters, and the fears some harbored about Jefferson, there was no violence. There was no need for military intervention and no judicial stalemate (as there would be in 2000). Our country proved itself more integrated than its factions and more stable as a result.

**Abolition.** The matter of slavery stained the first century of our national history, and its legacy has been a burden we've never lifted. The debate stretches back to before our Declaration and Constitution, and shaped many of the debates about our expansion, our commerce, and our interstate relations through the 1800s. Ultimately, it took a bloody, costly Civil War to end slavery. The end of slavery showed that we could strive for the "more perfect union" suggested in the Preamble of our Constitution. It overturned existing social orders and provided a fundamental challenge to our country—one that we survived. The result was one step forward in respecting all people, promoting dignity and equality, and recognizing a shared fortune for black and white in these United States.

**Breaking up the trusts.** "Trusts"—what an innocuous, almost positive name for the anticompetitive, anticonsumer monopolies created by big businesses to aggregate wealth. The extreme wealth stratification of the Gilded Age created a cadre of robber barons who controlled entire markets: steel, oil, railways. Not only were these trusts bad for business, they were bad for America. Teddy Roosevelt (and others, but he's most famously associated with this effort) became a "trust-buster," suing to break up these monopolies. He wanted a free market and saw these powerful figures as impeding this goal—so the government had a responsibility to be a tool that created a structure of fairness. When the government proactively intercedes for the greater good, as opposed to acting to protect the wealthy elites, we see America at its best.

289 **Women's suffrage.** It took us almost a century and a half before out country was able to see past "all men are created equal" to include all people. Half the population had been excluded from our political decisions: women, who ran households and businesses, formed communities and followed local issues, strengthened families and were every bit as entitled as any man to fair treatment. In 1920, the amendment guaranteeing women the right to vote was again proof that though it may be slow, the arc of history moves toward greater equality, inclusion, and respect.

290 **The New Deal.** It's hard to imagine what our country would be like without the reforms that elevated people out of poverty, regulated the greed of the banking industries (well, we've recently seen what life's like when banks go wild), and asserted that the federal government must play a role in shaping education and opportunity for all its citizens. Franklin Delano Roosevelt's advancements in the 1930s—joined later by Johnson's Great Society programs in the 1960s—created a network of safety nets, labor reforms, minimum wage, Social Security, and other pillars that have stabilized our society. Both sets of reforms asserted that we needed to tackle these problems together . . . and when the next great set of reforms expand health care to all and comprehensively transform our energy policy, they will be in the same lineage as these momentous agendas.

291 **Our entrance into World War II.** There have long been competing approaches to international relations in our country, a tension between those who support neutrality and isolation against those who support intervention and the exportation of democracy. It's not that one side is liberal or the other conservative. The approach—whether we go it alone or work with allies in the international community—is what makes it a liberal act. As do

our intentions: we are always acting for our own security, but are we also acting to amass wealth or to promote human rights, are we fighting to protect the powerful or defend the helpless?

In World War II, our struggle was not ours alone . . . in fact we were a little late to it. After Pearl Harbor, we saw that there was a struggle for peace and for rights, against aggression and against genocide, and we joined the European theater as well as the Pacific. We also understood that peace and security couldn't be left to one country alone—we had to work with allies to succeed in such a monumental effort. Investing in international, multi-lateral forces is a liberal approach to foreign policy, because it depends on seeing beyond our own self-interest. And, after the war, the creation of the United Nations was an effort to invest in a permanent structure of international collaboration.

**The aftermath of World War II: The Marshall Plan and the GI Bill.** World War II is a rich chapter in our history that makes all Americans proud. The aftermath of the war should compound that pride. Domestically, we passed a sweeping GI Bill that gave returning soldiers the opportunity for higher education. This expansive and expensive program ushered in an economic boom, created the workers needed for a new economy, and built a strong middle class—all because of redistribution of wealth through a government program. Internationally, the Marshall Plan to invest in the European countries that had just come through such a great conflict demonstrated our belief that spending large sums of money would pay back in peace and prosperity. Rather than exacting revenge for the war, or pulling back to our own isolating borders, we showed the world that we understood that we needed to look out for each other's interests and invest in each other's prosperity. We created a more stable, successful Europe as a result.

**Civil rights.** There are few Americans now who would openly argue against the right of a black person to vote, to shop at a restaurant, or to hold a job (though now those same prejudices sometimes exist toward immigrants). What a different America we were in the 1950s and 1960s, when students were barred from schools, and protestors were met with hoses and police dogs. Dramatic change in America never comes easily. We are fortunate that brave members of the civil rights movement, with effective leaders, focused strategies, and a passion for justice, dragged our country forward. If the struggle between conservative and liberal forces is characterized by status quo vs. change, authority vs. protest, self interest vs. communal good, the sanctity of individual preference vs. the embrace of a common goal, the civil rights movement showed that this can be a liberal country. Though there is always more work to do.

294

**The moon landing.** You might say that the dramatic events of 1969 which captured the world's imagination were the triumph of science, not liberalism. True—though we do need to remember that Bush administration right-wingers waged a war against science at every turn. The real reason to include this event is embodied in Neil Armstrong's famous words: "One small step for man, one giant leap for mankind." Armstrong was, perhaps inadvertently, creating what should become an enduring liberal slogan: embodying the fact that a greater good is often more remarkable than individual accomplishments. Truly, the moon landing was remarkable—and took place not because of independent entrepreneurship or innovation, but because of great communal effort, government resources, and common national purpose, set forth by President Kennedy's declaration at the start of the 1960s that by the end of the decade we'd put a man on the moon. It symbolizes what we are capable of when we invest in each other and in our country and when our country invests in us. All thanks to our socialized, big-government space program.

While the events above are generally agreed to be "Great Moments in American History," they also should be seen as examples of the collectivist, inclusive, diverse, and freethinking characteristics that shape a liberal vision of our country.

Furthermore, there are plenty of figures and incidents that embody an America we can be proud of that are not yet among our canon of "Great Moments." Here are a few I hope more high school history books will spend time praising in the future.

**Thoreau's antiwar activism.**  Henry David Thoreau is best known for *Walden*, his journal on living in the woods, embodying that American trope of self-reliance. What Thoreau is less noted for was his principled opposition to the Mexican War in the 1840s, an unnecessary war, sold on false premises by a conservative government looking to increase wealth for its most elite constituents. Sound familiar? Thoreau refused to pay taxes because he didn't wish to fund the war, and went to jail for it. That political dissent should be as discussed as his year in the woods.

295

**The achievements of Frances Perkins.**  Franklin Roosevelt's labor secretary, Perkins was the first woman to serve in the U.S. cabinet. She used that role as a powerful advocate for working families and was a critical partner in New Deal initiatives. She was the champion who helped pass progressive changes such as the minimum wage and overtime laws, which we still enjoy today.

296

**The repeal of Prohibition.**  It all comes back to the booze. In 1919, a puritanical streak in our country sparked an amendment to our Constitution prohibiting the manufacture and sale of alcohol. Thankfully, in 1933, Americans undid that decision. In addition to allowing for the creation of projects like Drinking Liberally, the repeal also sent an important message: Let's not create a culture of prohibition. Making behavior illegal often creates unregulated, dangerous underground networks and criminalizes our population. Within the law, risky behavior can be properly supervised and regulated, taxed for the common

297

good, and made safe for all. Ideally, that will someday extend to the more common and less harmful drugs that are prevalent in all walks of life in our country. Some celebrate December 5, the day the 21st Amendment repealed the 18th, as Repeal Day . . . a holiday we can all toast.

**298** **Loving v. Virginia.** In 1967, Mildred Delores Jeter and Richard Perry Loving came before the Supreme Court to petition for their right to marry. The aptly named "Loving" case ultimately overturned laws barring interracial marriage, a holdover from an earlier era. This decision brought us closer to being a country where all races are treated equally and where the mixing of people of different backgrounds is a strength. In Idaho Falls, local progressives from the Drinking Liberally chapter celebrate "Loving Day" as a chance to honor these liberal heroes. We hope this case will be fully honored in the history books of future generations.

**299** **The resignation of Richard Nixon.** This was a momentous event, but is often looked at as a sad moment for America. It seems to me to showcase America at its best.

If a liberal country believes that we share prosperity and purpose, then we also must share laws. Just as nobody—not even the largest trusts—may abuse our shared economy, nobody—not even the president—is above our common justice. Richard Nixon didn't believe that, as he demonstrated again and again in his actions. As he famously said in an interview several years after his presidency: "If the president does it, it isn't illegal."

Fortunately, our country proves again and again that when we make mistakes, we have ways to right them. In Nixon's case, we made the mistake of electing him twice, but we also made the more critical mistake of giving him enough latitude to abuse his power: to spy on political enemies, undercut democratic practices, and obstruct the processes of investigation and justice.

So we corrected it: proactive journalism followed by public organizing created pressure on Congress and a political climate in which Richard Nixon became the first president to step down in disgrace before the end of his term. As we had seen in 1800, we saw again in 1974 that the system can work, power can be transferred, no elite is enshrined, and the country is stronger than any one individual.

Very recently, Americans had the opportunity to add another mark to our liberal history: **the election of Barack Obama**. You don't have to like his policies, be a member of his party, or even have voted for him to recognize Obama's election as a remarkable moment in America. He is the face of the new American dream: interracial, with parents of diverse backgrounds, he grew from humble origins to take advantage of educational opportunities, give back to his community, come to serve as a representative, and then ascend to the presidency, reflecting the hopes of millions. Those that fear him most—like the "birthers" who challenge his citizenship—are really fearful that their country is changing: that new colors and names are emerging from a melting pot of languages and cultures. Liberals aren't scared, though: there is strength in our diversity. You see it in the new tone President Obama can strike when speaking to the Middle East and Africa. You see it in the disenfranchised communities that now believe they have a stake in the American project. We are a better country for our mixing of races, religions, ethnicities, and histories—by mixing, we share; by sharing, we strengthen. Our president now reflects that truth about America.

We will have to wait to learn whether history judges him a great president, and a liberal one . . . but his election itself was a remarkable feat in the pursuit of a better country.

In addition to the moments we celebrate, there are the myths we hear as well. It's not enough to embrace our liberal heritage;

we have to actively delete the conservative lies that threaten to distort our honest understanding of our country.

**Let's throw these conservative myths out of the history books.**

300 **It's not true that our founders were all slave owners.** Some people make the argument that nobody can be blamed for slavery since everyone was doing it. Thomas Jefferson embodies how complicated the case is: on one hand, trying to oppose slavery in the Declaration of Independence; on the other, being a slave owner himself. The fact is, though, that there were those who opposed slavery from the beginning, including Aaron Burr. We need to own up to our country's mistakes, and not allow ourselves to fall into the easy trap of assuming that because "everyone" was committing the same crime, that somehow made it OK. Only by acknowledging that even our greatest founders were guilty can we honestly assess and address the tensions built into our country.

301 **Actually, the yeoman farmer was not the ideal early American.** As much as liberals love Thomas Jefferson, he was guilty of a little rhetorical fraud. He was supposedly the champion of the yeoman farmer, the prototypical "rugged individual" that built our country. How did these farmers, pioneers, and trailblazers have land to explore? They were aided by the Louisiana Purchase, an unprecedented land deal that expanded the borders of our country. It was a huge government program presided over by President Thomas Jefferson and paid for by the national coffers, strengthened by commerce from the cities. As often happens throughout American history, the dreams of the individual are subsidized by the efforts of the government, paid for by our common wealth.

302 **False: Baseball was born in the countryside.** I love baseball. I grew up with all the myths about it: how it was created in the

innocent countryside, how it's always been a national booster in times of trouble, how teams have built up cities, and how the sport has supported America. However, we know that from the beginning, baseball was a business and the patriotic flag-waving has often been a marketing stunt. The greatest bit of public relations work had to do with the origins of the game. Before it was played by Abner Doubleday in the rolling hills of upstate New York farmland, it was played by immigrants and laborers in the streets of New York City. However, even then, the crowded, diverse cities somehow didn't sell as well as the images of rural, white America (or what Sarah Palin might call "real America"), so baseball businessmen made up a different story. We need to keep debunking such myths. We should restore city life as central to, not destructive of, American life. In the urban environments, resources are shared, classes mingle, and immigrants find a home. In cities, the American experiment is often at its most diverse, innovative, and successful.

**The 1950s were a time of great peace and prosperity . . . not quite.** There was a liberal consensus, a popular president, a booming economy—unless, of course, you were black. The 1950s may live on in our cultural imagination as *Leave it to Beaver*, but the serene surface masked deeper traumas: Jim Crow laws persevered. Violence against blacks was common and ignored. A conservative reading of history suggests that the civil rights movement created new problems that ruptured the beauty of the 1950s. In fact, the 1960s exposed tensions that were already there.

303

**No, Ronald Reagan did not end the Cold War.** Conservatives love Ronald Reagan, but his policies to consolidate wealth, bust unions, race-bait, and demonize social programs make him less loved among liberals. Boosters believe they have a trump card: the decline of the Soviet Union. But really the person who could take far more credit than Ronald Reagan is Mikhail Gorbachev, the Soviet premier. Pervasive structural problems

304

had weakened the Soviet economy before Reagan stepped into office, and that economic pressure opened the way for social pressures to liberalize the Soviet Union. Through his two policies of perestroika (reform) and glasnost (openness), Gorbachev courageously ushered in an era that would usher him out; he was a leader who took steps that would limit his own powers. Reagan just happened to be on the other side of the ocean.

## A "Liberal" Arts Education

Ideally, your high school education isn't only from textbooks, which tend to take the "story" out of "history." All students should graduate having read books that ask them to question what they learn, challenge authority, and make their own discoveries.

Below is a small selection of works that inspire and challenge, offer a view of another America that exists or could exist, and are just good reads. Many were, at one time, banned from schools, and some of them still are. Thankfully, a number of these books now appear in many high school curricula, reminding us that progress is possible.

**305** **1984.** George Orwell's compelling antiauthoritarian parable leaves you with chills as you contemplate how the examples of "Big Brother" in today's world try to force us into silence and conformity.

**306** **Catch-22.** War may be absurd, not just glorious. The retelling of it can make you laugh and cry at once. Joseph

Heller's acclaimed novel asks us to take a new look at old battles and gives us a shared language to despise senseless bureaucracy.

**The Grapes of Wrath.** An argument by the great John Steinbeck that when people struggle, not only do they need the kindness of others, they also need large-scale reform that we can only provide together.

307

**Slaughterhouse-Five.** Kurt Vonnegut's most lasting novel describes his experience witnessing America firebomb a city during World War II . . . and the time- and space-traveling fantasy that allows him to deal with the horror. Plus it's really funny.

308

**No Name in the Street.** James Baldwin's essays, written after he decided to return from his successful expatriate days in Europe to the civil rights–era South, address his struggle to define American identity and ask the reader to struggle as well.

309

**To Kill a Mockingbird.** Harper Lee creates the enduring protagonist of a young girl who learns not to judge people based on race or fears or that which divides us. The novel offers a picture of a different era of racial bigotry in America, and some sad lessons on what happens when justice isn't served.

310

**Fahrenheit 451.** Ray Bradbury's tale of a society in which a "fireman" is a book-burner. After you read it, check out BannedBooksWeek.org and find something to read that's still being banned in America today.

311

**Beloved.** This work won Toni Morrison the Pulitzer Prize and is President Obama's favorite novel. Yet this story about the brutality of slavery and the challenge of building a life after escaping from it continues to be removed from school library shelves for its language and violence. Read a banned book . . . it will also give you something to discuss with the president.

**The Shock Doctrine.** Naomi Klein's assessment of the interlocking power grabs, vast profits, and wars that have shaped global dynamics for the past forty years will make you rethink what you've learned in history class.

**A People's History of The United States** by Howard Zinn. Because there's more truth than in our current history books.

## Reading Liberally

We may challenge our educational upbringing, but we cannot change or erase it entirely. Therefore, we need to focus on what we can do in our daily lives to continue to learn liberally. Where do we go for information? How do we filter, and whom should we trust? If conservative bias is deep in our cultural psyche, will we be able to recognize it?

The short answer: there is no right answer. As the great liberal American poet Walt Whitman suggested, "listen to all sides and filter them from yourself." You should take healthy skepticism and scrutiny into all lessons. Talk out your thoughts or confusions with others. A benefit of a liberal community is that you have more people to bounce ideas off.

A good starting place, though, is to read. There's a reason you get more out of what you read than what you watch or hear: TV and radio set their own pace; in reading, you set the pace. You can return to a question, underline a thought, stop and pick up again later. TV and radio exist in time; texts exist outside of time and allow you to engage with them when and how you want.

317

So, what should you read?

## Magazines

In addition to a newspaper, why not try a few magazines?

318

★ It's hard to be a daily paper. It's a constant race to keep up with deadlines, which means depth is sometimes sacrificed for immediacy. The pressure to boost sales often pushes sensationalism to the fore-front. Magazines have the time to dig more deeply, and more thoughtfully, to offer longer articles with more nuanced themes.

★ Magazines support investigative journalism. In some ways, with news, we get what we pay for. In an era of free media, there might not be funding for as much deep, probing journalism as our democracy deserves. Magazines are not always a solution—but in the run-up to the Iraq war, the revelations of torture, the concerns about a neoconservative push to militarily engage Iran, magazines were at the forefront of these stories. We need investigative journalists, so we need to help support institutions that pay them.

★ Magazines are sharable. Sure, you might pass on a newspaper in the course of an afternoon, but it's old news by the next day. The longer shelf life of a magazine makes it more likely you'll pass it along and be able to engage in substantive conversations with neighbors or colleagues about what you read.

319 Which magazines? Go explore a newspaper stand and find some you like . . . but here are a few suggestions:

320 **Mother Jones,** a Bay Area–based publication, is a clear alternative to mainstream media. While many newspapers choose to cover the same stories as each other, in a race to conformity, in *Mother Jones* you're more like to find a piece that will challenge the norms.

321 **The Nation** for well over a century has been a constant progressive voice, and in its pages creates space for vibrant political discourse, including divergent views within the left.

322 **The New Yorker.** I used to think *The New Yorker* was a fashionable accessory for people who wanted to demonstrate they lived among an intellectual upper crust. Turns out that I was being a jerk. *The New Yorker* breaks stories, and gives more pages

to serious topics than newspapers can afford. Each week, its lengthy articles give you a chance to explore issues you may not have considered and give you the terms and tools to make sense of those topics.

Do you need to have subscriptions to all these? No, of course not. There's also the guilt felt by most subscribers that they don't get to read each issue, and the piles of untouched magazines grow in the corner of your home, a reminder of your personal failings.

Fortunately, that's what public libraries are for. Go on in and leaf through a magazine. Pick up some conservative rags as well—it's worth knowing their arguments in order to make ours stronger.

One tip for when you're done reading a liberal magazine, and this comes from John Javna's *50 Simple Things You Can Do to Fight the Right*: leave the magazine out and open on a library table. For one, when librarians clear up after you, it shows them that people were reading *Mother Jones*, and makes them more likely to renew the subscription or mention to other librarians that it's a popular title.

Second, when you leave a magazine out and open, you never know who might come by to pick it up. You may have just lured someone new into Reading Liberally.

## Books

You can bring more than magazine advocacy to your local library. Organize in order to use your library's purchasing power to push all manner of published progressivism. Research what titles are being released and drop a note for your librarian. Ask ten friends to request it. Libraries work on a very local level, and many librarians have a good amount of discretion in what they purchase. They want to buy what will be read—if it is of value to their customers, it is of value to their institution. Create a market for the next titles by progressive radio personalities like Tom Hartmann, or new releases from an independent, progressive publisher like Ig Publishing. The library is going to spend its money somewhere; it might as well support publishers that support good work.

You can also become your own library. Anytime you own a book, think about its fate. Should it be exiled to a pile or a high shelf dusty with years of accumulation? Instead, is there a way the book can live on? Lending libraries and book swaps are organized grassroots avenues to give that book new purpose. Pass a book along to friends, or set up a swap with your neighbors or carpoolers. One nice touch is to put a name and date on the inside back cover; if you feel really forward, include contact info as well. As the book lives again and again in new hands, there's something amusing about seeing where it's been. You never know when you may want to talk to somebody about it, and there's a list of people you could e-mail.

**Reading groups.** The desire to talk about books and share the experience of reading is behind the proliferation of book clubs nationwide. We are part of this trend with Reading Liberally book groups. There are many of us who fondly remember discussions sections from college and miss the ability to trade ideas in our grown-up life. There are others who read something and don't know what to do next. They desire a community to help them make sense of the book and think about its consequences. You have other folks as well who only read if they're given a deadline. Whatever reason, a book club is a simple way to make the individual act of reading into a shared act of community building.

When we started Reading Liberally chapters, we provided recommendations of books that we thought groups would enjoy. We quickly remembered liberals don't like to march in lockstep.

While we thought it would be cool if dozens of chapters read the same book to be part of a national discussion, each group quickly made clear they had their own interests and considerations. Fair enough—they are stronger as a result of being self-organized.

The amusing part is that the hosts who rebelled against our push for conformity soon found the tables turned. When local Reading Liberally organizers suggested books for their own members to read, they got push-back from members demanding to know why they should all read the same book within the club. Why not choose a theme, suggest a few readings, and let anyone then read whatever they wanted, bringing more information and a wider array of insights into the conversation? Herding liberals is never easy.

Whether you choose one book together, or have people bring in different source materials, there are some simple steps to liberalize your local literary crew.

**Choose something the library stocks.**  Not everyone wants to buy a book each month, and you don't want to lose members over that. Make your selection something available at the local library. This will keep more members engaged, and will send the librarians a message about what people are reading.

330

**Support liberal publishers.**  Liberal books are published by major companies when they are written by big names like Al Franken or a Kennedy. There are many other strong, interesting liberal voices that aren't yet known quantities and major publishers might not take the risk. Smaller publishing houses like Chelsea Green, a Vermont-based publisher best known for food and environmental works, and Ig Publishing, a Brooklyn business that's been turning bloggers into print authors, present terrific work that just doesn't get around as much. Help spread the word and keep these publishers in business.

331

**Don't be too dry.** There is an endless number of good policy works out there, but reading only policy is a quick way to lose steam. While a work on climate change followed by a tome on health policy followed by a discourse on education would be valuable, it may also be dull. Mix in fiction, memoirs, poetry. Keep your selections varied and fresh, and that will keep the conversation lively and the group going strong.

**Make everyone the decider.** Some book clubs attempt to find consensus each month. Unfortunately, that can lead to less inspired choices and fewer risks. What if each month you pass the decision-making power to a different member? You'll receive a wider range of choices and a few surprises. These selections may be less well known but quite worth the risk. Plus, everyone becomes an owner of the club—in addition to choosing a book, everyone leads discussions, prepares questions or thoughts, does supplementary research. Groups are stronger when everyone contributes.

**Mix in some living authors.** One could read for years from the great works of the past: from Frederick Douglass to John Steinbeck, Elizabeth Cady Stanton to Upton Sinclair. By all means, steep yourself in that history. Also, though, consider the added benefits of living authors. By buying their books, you're supporting and encouraging them, and by reading their works, you have more opportunity to join in a current dialogue. You might be able to reach out to them directly, or see them speak. Fundamentally, you become part of a movement that keeps them producing and keeps fostering new liberal views and voices.

One last note for a liberal book club: food . . . and drink. Do it potluck—from each according to his ability, to each according to his appetite.

**Host an author.**  In addition to a regular club that meets at cafés or homes, Reading Liberally also hosts authors on tours. Many progressive authors would love to connect to a live audience, and outside a few major cities, many don't have networks that can host them. Getting into a new city has value for them—it might give them an excuse to get on area radio or in the local paper, it may create buzz among local bloggers, and it might sell some books. They also, honestly, just enjoy knowing that people care about their work.

You don't need to be a major organization to host authors. Why not reach out to them, and give it a try? What do you have to lose? It's easy to do:

★ Write to them through their websites or publishers.

★ Be clear with them about expectations. What type of event are you inviting them to? How many people might be there?

★ Offer more help, if you can. Can you send press releases to the local paper, or make introductions to the local radio station? Can you get an event scheduled at a bookstore? These are good incentives, but offer only if you can really follow through.

★ Start local. Many authors have no travel budget, so start with folks who might be a short commute away. See which local faculty members at area colleges have recently published books.

And yes . . . all of these tricks would work on me. If you throw in a free dinner and beer, I'm definitely there.

## The Internet

There's more information in the world than is printed on dead trees. While books give you longer views and deeper insights, the web is more likely your immediate source for news. The internet has unparalleled power to connect you with stories and voices around the world and to give you up-to-the moment coverage, commentary, audio, and video. The internet breaks any monopoly a few agencies can have on the news by empowering anyone and everyone to publish their own news and opinions. By opening the gates wide to people with a range of experiences and expertise, theoretically we could find more accurate information than we could from a few channels and a handful of papers.

Then there is the fear that we could get more inaccuracies; that a world without formal editors and publishers is a world without standards. There is such a glut of information, how do you find what's most important?

Those are legitimate concerns, but surmountable ones. The fact is that our professional papers with publishers and editors get things wrong, as do well-known encyclopedias. Print media has its corporate ties to deal with, and every profession is at risk of groupthink.

The online encyclopedia, Wikipedia, has addressed these challenges and become a trusted source for information. That's not saying you should trust everything on those pages, but there is a community built around the site that monitors it for quality.

Wikipedia is like any common resource: if anyone poisons it, nobody can use it; but if everyone participates, contributes to, and protects it, we all benefit. As with any research you do, don't assume everything on Wikipedia is accurate.

Take similar caution when reading blogs, and you will be able to put similar faith in them. There are inaccuracies, there are agendas, there are opinions disguised as coverage and pay-for-play alliances unannounced. All of that exists on the NBC nightly news as well, so as with any information, you just have to figure out whom to trust.

For example, if you read the *New York Times*, you decide there are some columnists you tend to believe more than others. You draw that conclusion after reading them over time, considering their arguments, weighing them against information you learn, and deciding who seems trustworthy.

The same standard applies to blogs. Take recommendations from friends you trust. Read a handful and question what they tell you. Make blogs earn your loyalty. When you do find someone who gets it right consistently, see whom he or she trusts by seeing who they link to.

Online media may feel fresh and seem to break the mold, but the ground rules are basically the same. If someone regularly publishes false reports, stop reading them and tell other people to stop reading them too.

Once you feel confident enough to stray from the major media websites, you will discover great sources for liberal perspectives on the day's events.

**Daily Kos.**  This high-traffic progressive blog is loved and loathed by political allies and enemies respectively. Kos has more readers than many daily papers, and among the audience are influential readers: policy makers, advocates, elected officials.

Kos, short for the site's founder "Markos," is a community blog. Anyone can sign up for an account and publish diaries on any

341

subject they please. Only a handful of authors have "front page" privileges to create the content that regularly appears on the first page of the website. All other diaries, though, still have a home: they are listed in a side column on the front page. Readers can "recommend" diaries, helping keep the posts on the front page longer.

This system enables independent authors to develop followings. Some writers focus on particular topics and become trusted on specific issues. Others become known for their tone. Hundreds of regular readers comment on all the posts, joining and enlarging the conversation.

While most posts offer analysis or opinion, Daily Kos will at times provide original coverage; it regularly offers videos; and it also conducts independent professional polling.

342 **Think Progress.** A project of the Center for American Progress, a Washington, D.C.–based think tank, this site is more news than opinion. It chooses news stories that focus on a liberal agenda: exposing the hypocrisy of the right, discussing movement on progressive initiatives and conservative obstacles. The stories are presented factually and are well resourced, and these posts frequently cover topics that may be overlooked in the general press.

343 **Talking Points Memo** proved that a website could also conduct real investigative journalism. Founded by a former traditional media journalist, TPM was a leader in making a real story out of the U.S. Attorney firings. TPM proved that you didn't need heavy printing machinery to be a vital source of news.

344 **FireDogLake,** or FDL as it is colloquially called, empowers its readers to become activist journalists. Readers call and confront members of Congress to create public records of where those representatives stand on different issues. The site is an activist

hub and a news source, ensuring its readers have the best information to act as the best advocates.

**Jack & Jill Politics** brings a black political voice to the topics of the day. Mixing humor and style into their writing, J&J has become an important vehicle for black perspectives, which are often missing from media coverage—even when discussing issues involving the black community.

**Empty Wheel.** Marcy Wheeler, the author of this blog, was the authority on the Plame affair and Libby trial, and since then has been recognized with prestigious journalism awards. She's proof that blogs are more than self-interested unemployed recent college grads in their bathrobes.

**Feministing** offers a young, hip, feminist view on the world of politics and on the portrayal and continued stereotypes of women in society. A good source for stories of overt sexism, and a great source of enjoyable reading.

**Open Left** is a progressive strategy blog, discussing how to move forward a left-leaning agenda. This site is far from serving as a Democratic mouthpiece. Open Left writers spend more time confronting conservative and compromising Dems for selling their party and supporters short than they do criticizing Republicans, whose right-wing leanings aren't worth arguing against.

**FiveThirtyEight** became a phenomenon in the lead-up to the '08 election as a smart, focused, exciting site about polling. It took its name from the total number of electoral votes. FiveThirty Eight gave number-lovers something to feast on each day and continues to analyze polls, votes, and current races.

**Crooks and Liars** is your go-to place for video. You can find the best clips from the TV talk shows (without having to suffer through the entire programs) and the best videos being

345

346

347

348

349

350

produced by progressive groups. It's the television channel of the movement.

**351**    **Eschaton** is whip-fast rapid response of biting snark hitting all the events of the news cycle. And Atrios, the founder and chief blogger, is a regular Liberal Drinker.

**352**    **Living Liberally.** While our main focus is bringing people into face-to-face communities, we blog as well. "Screening Liberally Big Picture" and "Reading Liberally Page Turner" columns offer cultural reviews through a liberal lens. "Laughing Liberally to Keep From Crying" gives you the comedic turn on the day, "Drinking Liberally Shot of Truth" talks about the strength of social bonds in the progressive movement, and "Eating Liberally Food for Thought" connects food and politics.

There are two features of blogs that far surpass traditional news. One, they actively reference each other. In the blogosphere, any one blog is stronger because so many other blogs exist. That's how they generate audiences and build stories. Blogs look out for each other.

Second, readers can participate. Letters to the editor are an established way to voice opinion, but there are inherent limits to how many can be published. On many blogs—like Eschaton—the commentary is often longer than the original posts, and the empowered readers come to know and trust each other as a community.

**353**    Don't just read blogs—join them. Add your voice, challenge the assumptions, and share your knowledge. You will discover entire online communities where you feel at home.

**354**    Then, share what you learn. An advantage of electronic media: you don't need a lending library to pass along your findings. Send an e-mail. Friends may read what you forward them because they trust you. Send them interesting posts, and you'll become their trusted source.

## Television

TV has obvious imperfections as a source of good information. Commercial pressures get in the way of important discussions. News shows that are more entertaining—with bright lights, dramatic music, attractive anchors, and conjured controversy— make more money. Fox News proves that point.

However, for many people, TV is going to shape how they view the world. So how do you engage someone who is learning televisedly, to encourage them to learn liberally?

**Encourage them to change the channel.** Unless they're PBS junkies, they're probably not absorbing too much "must-see" television. Channel surfing is a good way to shake up perspectives. You see that CNN covers something differently than MSNBC, or that the shrill urgency of cable news is a different tone than the comparable calm of the network evening news. People should have more than one source of news, and suggesting that someone switch around is an easy way to shake them up.

**Ask them to identify the channel's bias.** If bias is too strong a word, ask what the "angle" is. People pretty much accept that very few reports are totally objective. Urging friends to think about the subjectivity of news coverage—who the channels may be protecting, why some industries are targets and others are not, whether the station has interests other than telling the news—is a good way to subtly challenge the information they're getting.

**Give them a magazine.** You're not going to break their TV habit, but you can work around it. Give them a week-old magazine, highlight a story of interest, and make it easy for them to get more than one perspective.

## Talking Liberally

Where you gather your news is important, but real learning happens through interaction. Who do you speak with? Who are you influencing? How are you influencing them? Are you making the most of each opportunity?

Often the people most comfortable discussing politics are the people most confident in their views. That's unfortunate. Those people may be overconfident because they see the world in black-and-white and don't tolerate nuance. This may make them short-tempered with people who are still discovering their views. This may make them especially loud, and have a silencing effect on those around them. This doesn't lead to good discussion.

While these overbearing folks tend to be blustery, demagogic right-wingers, we on the left have our share of shouters. They're not out to discuss, engage, or convince; they lecture and rant. While I can respect the passion of such voices on both sides, this is not the best way to draw new people into political discussion, much less persuade them.

Studies show the greatest determinant of your likelihood to vote is whether someone has asked you to. Someone personally inviting you into a process is more effective than ads and news stories declaring that an election is important. Similarly, young people vote for the first time because somebody took the time to ask their opinion. Young people are often topics of political conversations, but less frequently participants in those same debates. When someone asks them about their views and connects the issues they care about with the political process, they do vote. Furthermore, if you vote once, you're more likely to vote regularly and develop a lifelong voting habit.

Therefore, it is important to talk politics with regular voters and new ones. Old dogs can learn new tricks. Conservatives can change their minds. They are not going to switch stripes because of a *New York Times* editorial. They are going to do it because personal experiences and appeals ask them to view the world in a new light. So if we want to liberalize the country, we have to start locally, by liberalizing those around us.

The responsibility is yours. You have to bring politics to the dinner table. You have to question your friends. You have to engage your conservative relatives.

358
359
360

361

## Talk Liberally With Non-liberals.

It can be fun to talk with people who agree with you and, honestly, we do that at Drinking Liberally. Ultimately, those conversations should lead to you having the confidence to engage non-liberals as well. No conservative is ever going to change his mind if all he hears is what other conservatives have to say. We are the side of inclusion, engagement, and the belief that we're all in this together—that means we have to live those values in our own conversations. If we believe in a foreign policy of engaging hostile nations, then certainly we can engage ornery conservatives.

**Don't shout.** We get that you might be right and they might be wrong, but starting a conversation with that is the surest route to ending it right away.

**Respect them.** You may not agree with their opinions, but if you are engaging someone, you probably have some respect for them. Express that respect: listen to them, don't condescend, and let them know that your respect is why you're having this discussion.

**Be willing to disagree.** Friends and family do not always feel comfortable contradicting each other too blatantly. This can lead to a lot of "No, no, I agree," and "I think we're saying the same thing." If you were really saying the same thing, you wouldn't be having the discussion. Make clear that it is not a crime to disagree. You may want the same end, or share values, but you may differ nonetheless. Only by pointing out those differences will there be room to learn and convince.

**Make it personal.** Your conservative friend is listening to you. They are not watching Rachel Maddow or reading *The Nation*. There is a personal bond that has drawn them into the conversation, and some amount of trust. Don't quote statistics that you're regurgitating from an online poll. Talk to them about your values, feelings, and experiences. Share anecdotes from the lives of your friends to demonstrate points about rights for gays and lesbians, the need for health care, the challenges faced by working families. Antigay discrimination will cease someday not because we legislate against it or because celebrities challenge it but because everyone will eventually know and love a gay friend or family member. In issue after issue, if you can make it personal, you can at least budge people from their lockstep conservatism.

**Do it at a dinner table.** "No talk of politics, religion, or sex at the table" seems to be a rule for polite company. Like the rule against ending sentences with prepositions, it's a rule I refuse to subscribe to. First of all, what's left to talk about—the weather? Second, if you don't talk politics with people with whom you're willing to break bread, then you'll only get it dished out by professional reporters and commentators, and that's just not good enough. At a dinner table, people are together long enough to have a real conversation. This should give you time to talk and to listen.

At Drinking Liberally, sharing a pint—or even better, a pitcher—ensures the conversation continues until the drinks are drained.

## Parenting Liberally

There are some audiences who have no choice but to dine with you: your children. If you are a parent, you are making choices that influence your kids all the time, and those choices teach them liberal attitudes from an early age.

There is no question that I learned liberal values from my family. I went to a cooperative preschool where parents volunteered one day a week. We all came to know each other's moms and dads from an early age and called them all by first names, creating an egalitarian spirit that made it easier to question them, learn from them, and, as I got older, debate with them.

We had a closet full of costumes in my house, inviting me to be creative and invent my own stories. From theater games to a video camera, there was always incentive to improvise, to become comfortable speaking and sharing. There was also ample opportunity to "produce"—live productions, videos, elaborate adventures. I quickly learned that I couldn't produce alone and discovered the joys of collaboration.

There were no rules limiting the number of friends who could come over after school. So while some friends had to choose two or three playmates when they invited us over, I was allowed to invite anyone and everyone, a lesson in inclusion.

When my friends weren't around, my parents were, and they were playmates to me as well. We read more than a dozen *Wizard of Oz* books aloud as long as I would write down every word I didn't know the meaning of and promise to look it up or ask what it meant.

In addition to storytelling, Mom and Dad included us in conversations of all kinds. I remember talking politics at the dinner table, learning from my parents about what was happening in the world. It was never as formal as a lesson-of-the night. They would simply ask us what was going on in our lives and share what was happening in theirs. They believed children should be seen and heard.

I am not yet able to speak from the perspective of a parent about raising a child with liberal values . . . fortunately, I was able to turn to the two best experts I know: my parents. They brought me to a Walter Mondale rally at age six, encouraged my student activism in middle school and high school, and taught me that I had a responsibility to care about the world. And it turns out they have a few ideas about parenting.

## Tips for Parenting Liberally

### Written with guest contributors Suzanne Karp Krebs and Eric Krebs (Mom and Dad)

**Create a participatory home.** If you want to raise children with the belief that we all are in this world together, then you need to reflect that lesson in your home. Have your children participate in family discussions and decisions, whether that's planning a vacation or deciding what charities to support. The process does not need to be pure democracy, but ask their views and explain your decisions. Additionally, include them in family responsibilities, setting up chores so they understand how they contribute to the common good of the household. Bring them to your office, and share your hobbies, so they are familiar with your life.

365

As you involve them in the household, in return you need to participate in their lives. Meet their friends and friends' parents; attend their sporting events, school productions, and group activities; and offer to coach, drive, and support them when you can. Be involved in their education at school and at home by meeting their teachers, joining the Parent-Teacher Association at school, and helping them with their homework. You should give your kids room to learn and play on their own, but by encouraging everyone to participate in each other's lives, you teach them how you hope they will engage with the world.

366

367

368

One more great example of this participatory spirit is collective child care. For people who can't afford preschool, setting up a child care collective is another way to build a supportive network around your children. As Hillary Clinton wrote, "It takes a village . . ."

369

While inclusive, group experiences are great, don't forget to spend quality one-on-one time with your child as well. Find activities you and she share, just the two of you.

370

**Encourage exploration.** John Dewey was an educator and philosopher who laid out a vision for what a liberal education should look like. Children needed to be given opportunities to try, fail, and learn from failure; they needed to be encouraged to think creatively, not memorize by rote; they needed experiences that challenged them and left them with a sense of navigating the complexity of the real world, not simply academic tasks.

371

This is more than theory. It plays out in some of the best schools and childhood experiences you can imagine. As federal funding pushes more schools to put pressure on test scores, it can be harder to create these alternative, authentic assessments in the classroom, making it even more important that such creative, risk-taking exploration happen outside the school day.

Giving children freedom does not mean always saying yes. Children need boundaries and structure (one wishes that the titans of Wall Street who tossed our economy into crisis knew a little more about "boundaries"). Limiting television time will teach a child to make choices and will keep him from becoming an addict. When you say "no" to your children, explain why. They might resent the decision, but, over time, they will feel respected.

**Tell stories.** Storytelling excites the imagination and encourages expression. It also can be a way to cultivate compassion, empathy, and community spirit at an early age. The stories we tell have morals. They teach us to trust, to help one another, to build community, to develop values other than love of money, and to sacrifice for a common good.

**Share your values.** If you want your children to embrace values of inclusion, diversity, charity, compassion, and free expression, you need to lead by example and demonstrate those values. However, it's not enough to do good. Take a moment to discuss your choices. Talk to your kids about the environment, and what you all can do as a family to conserve energy and reduce waste. When you participate in community service, give to a charity, or vote, explain why these causes are important.

Furthermore, do not hesitate to discuss the values you see your children demonstrating in their behavior. If you do not like how they are treating other children, tell them. Being honest with your children about their behavior is still a way of showing your love, and will educate them on how to be kind and inclusive to others.

**Encourage play. . . . and fair play.**  Being playful is a virtue in itself, and a generation that grows up joyful is a generation that will spread its joy to others around the world. What and how we play also teach us values. It's common to say that sports encourage teamwork, discipline, strategic thinking. All games teach some lessons, some more profound than others. Think about what those lessons are.

379

Choose games that teach inclusion, where every kid has a role and kids with different skills can contribute. The activities can still be competitive, and teams can win and lose, but you want to make sure everyone is learning from those experiences.

380

Encourage collaborative activities where kids can work together. Whether these are puzzles, scavenger hunts, or competitive team-based games like Capture the Flag or charades, they teach children to work together and trust each other. Find games that inspire creative thinking . . . after all, we need liberals to be able to creatively solve the problems we're inheriting from the right wing.

381

382

**Start early.**  It's never too early in a child's life to learn love, compassion, and inclusion, or to learn that reading is more thought-provoking than watching television, or to understand that waste isn't a virtue. And as soon as your kid talks, ask what she's thinking and feeling. Listen. Respect. Share. Engage. It's easier to do now than to have to wait and engage a conservative uncle at the Thanksgiving table.

383

## Everything I Need to Know for a Liberal Life I Learned in Kindergarden

★ Kids who hoard toys are jerks.

★ 2 + 2 = 4, regardless of what a math-denier says.

★ If you pollute our milk and cookies with excess greenhouse gases, we all lose.

★ Muppets of all colors can love each other.

★ Simply having more cookies than everyone else doesn't make you cool or happy; sharing them with everyone else does.

### And the Liberal Moral of the Story Is . . .

If you want to raise little liberals, encourage them to pick up books that will cultivate a sense of inquiry and independence, compassion and wonder. Here are a few suggestions for their recommended reading list . . . or to read out loud with them.

**The Lorax.** This Dr. Seuss fable tells the story of the ultimate environmentalist—the Lorax, who speaks for the trees. An unfortunate fate meets the forest and its inhabitants when nobody listens to his message. The result is a basic lesson in conservation, tucked into a colorful, comical, creative tale.

**The Harry Potter Books.**  One of the most successful series of all time, these books are thick with liberal lessons. In these tales — which are addictive, watch out — you learn to trust people who aren't like you, to believe that people of mixed backgrounds can embody the best of both worlds, and that everyone — even a house elf — deserves to pursue his dreams. A few avid readers even turned activist and formed an organization called "The HP Alliance" that has created social action around the morals of the story: they have conducted campaigns against genocide in Darfur and for tolerance and diversity in America.

385

**Free to Be You and Me.**  "I find everyone I know who was raised on this book is well adjusted," observes Eating Liberally founder Kerry Trueman. This book-album tag-team teaches you about embracing differences, encourages you to love yourself, and prepares you to love others.

386

**The poetry of Shel Silverstein.**  Whether creating a band out of playing your belly, or telling the story of Hector the Collector's lovely junk collection, poems from *Where the Sidewalk Ends* and *A Light in the Attic* cultivate a sense of whimsy, playfulness, and the belief that anything is possible. They create a beautiful world, made magical by exploration, collaboration, and appreciation.

387

**The Encyclopedia Brown** series about a reality-based boy detective who investigates, exposes irrational inconsistencies, and beats bad guys with logic.

388

**Blubber,** by Judy Blume, is a classic coming-of-age story that makes a case for ignoring the mob and learning empathy.

389

**The Lord of the Rings trilogy.**  A fellowship of underdogs, across race, sets aside differences to topple totalitarianism.

390

**The Little Prince.** The children's book for all ages, that simply, thoughtfully, and creatively reminds us to be good in the world, to take responsibility, and to open our hearts.

# Religion

I grew up in a Reform Jewish household, and there are some proud liberal elements to that religion. Israel literally means "one who wrestles with God," and Jews are encouraged to wrestle with ideas and authority. Even traditional Judaism encourages debate, and more modern strains assume that today's Jews will be finding their own ways to continue traditions in a modern world.

Most faiths have liberal traditions within them. Catholicism has often been a major force in caring for the poor. Unitarianism, the church in which Ralph Waldo Emerson practiced, was a voice for abolitionism in the mid-1800s, and has been a model of tolerance for people of different faiths throughout its history. Quakers are leaders in antiwar activities. Islam has been an engine of science and learning and has an emphasis on charity and hospitality. Even religions that seem more conservative are never monolithic. Increasingly, younger evangelicals are participating in the environmental movement. More Protestant faiths are accepting gay and lesbian ministers.

Furthermore, even within conservative religious contexts, people find ways to be faithful to their church and to their political beliefs. There are Catholic churches that embrace their homosexual members openly. There are conservative synagogues that welcome their interfaith congregants with open arms. You just have to know how to look for the right congregations.

# Take It from a Rabbi . . .

I do not participate in organized religion in an everyday way . . . so I turned to an expert for her advice: Hayley Siegel, a friend and rabbinic student at the Academy for Jewish Religion, a pluralistic, nondenominational seminary. Hayley suggests a few areas where a congregation can live up to its responsibilities in an interdependent, inclusive world. While these questions are posed to Jewish synagogues, you can easily translate to other faiths and congregations.

## Environmental

★ Does the synagogue serve as a site for a CSA? Increasingly, synagogue members are even organizing their own food co-ops for kosher/organic meat, veggies, and fruit. 392

★ What kind of "green" initiatives does the synagogue implement? Do they provide members with bike racks? Does the shul have energy-efficient appliances? Are they planning any initiatives to reduce waste/pollution? 393

★ Do they procure foods or materials for holidays, bat and bar mitzvahs, and weddings from local vendors? 394

## Liturgical/Prayer

★ Do their prayer books use gender-neutral pronouns in the liturgy? Do they not refer to "God" as "King" or "He"? 395

★ Do they accept women and gay/lesbian congregants on the bimah as rabbis and cantors?

## Economic

★ Does the synagogue pay all its workers a living wage?

## Social

★ Does the synagogue organize service projects that might help a broader community outside their neighborhood, such as travel to New Orleans?

★ Do they have an usher volunteer exchange program with a church, through which Christian ushers help out during the Jewish High Holidays, and Jews help out during Christmas?

## Intermarriage

★ Does the synagogue have an inclusive policy and attitude toward intermarriage and non-Jewish spouses? What kind of a role does the non-Jewish spouse play within the synagogue? Can he/she vote in synagogue-wide elections? May he/she participate during the child's bar/t mitzvah? Will the rabbi officiate at an intermarriage and, if so, what are the terms?

Many people find in their religion the type of community I find in liberalism—so it's important to find the places where religion promotes liberal values and where today's liberal lifestyle can be incorporated into traditional religious institutions. Whatever your religion, here are a few general questions you can ask to decide if your liberal and religious life can coexist.

**Does the congregation respect non-congregants?** It almost seems obvious in today's world that religions respect one another, but that isn't always the case. Some churches will discourage you from fraternizing with people outside the faith, or will continue to condemn those who aren't believers. There isn't room for that anymore. Churches that actively participate in interfaith dialogues have more to offer to our modern America.

401

**Does the congregation respect gender equality?** Our government finally gave women the right to vote ninety years ago, but we're still fighting for equal wages and other equal protections. Religion is a moral leader in the cause for equality. Any church that doesn't fully respect its women is far behind the times.

402

**Does the congregation respect gay and lesbian members?** It's heart-breaking to hear stories of men and women who grow up in a religion, who consider it their community and core to their values, and then are told they're not welcome anymore. While not every religion yet recognizes full marriage equality, every faith has more progressive denominations that clearly embrace their gay and lesbian brothers and sisters.

403

**Does the congregation invest in the neighboring community?** Churches have long been leaders in efforts to run shelters, feed and clothe the poor, protect the environment, and provide educational and athletic opportunities. These activities build community in the neighborhood of the congregation, lending important credibility to local efforts.

404

**Does the congregation celebrate?** Again, we look back to *Footloose* and the idea of a minister against dancing. As famed progressive leader Emma Goldman once said, "If I can't dance, I don't want to be part of your revolution." The same should be said of religion. Churches are meant to appeal to the highest elements of our soul, to reveal the beauty of the world. This should occur through song and dance, community meals and festivals. If not, then what's the point?

Finally, there are ways to participate in faith outside a congregation. Many of us celebrate holidays outside formal services. We gather with our families, exchange gifts, and leisurely enjoy the day. You don't need a congregation to be liberal on your behalf. Holidays are great opportunities to live the belief that we are all living for each other and not for ourselves alone. Donate to food and clothing drives. Consider giving to charities in your loved one's name rather than giving him or her a gift. Volunteer at soup kitchens or shelters on holidays, when the needy may be feeling particularly lonely. Shop consciously for gifts that support local craftspeople and artists and cut down on waste. And make sure to show goodwill to all. That's the most liberal and religious action you can take.

# CHAPTER 6
# SPENDING
# LIBERALLY

*Liberals feel unworthy of their*
*possessions. Conservatives feel they*
*deserve everything they've stolen.*
—MORT SAHL

Recently, the "No Impact Family" sought to bring their environmental impact as close to zero as possible, while still living a full life in New York City. They gave up take-out, bought from the local farmers' market, and skipped items that had unnecessary wrapping. They reused bags, stopped riding cars and subways, and turned off their electricity. What this experiment, and the book and movie that document it, proved was not that it's easy or even possible to eliminate all impact—but that you can find ways in which every facet of your life can be made healthier, more sustainable, and less commercial.

"No Impact Man" conducted an extreme and exciting experiment, but you don't need to live at an extreme to live liberally. You may start by spending less and by spending more consciously.

We only vote on Election Day. Daily we endorse elements of the world around us by voting with our dollars. Let's spend that money on businesses and industries that invest in the community. Spend in ways that green our planet, rather than blacken it, and that reward trust and compassion, not commercialism and greed.

Are you ready to spend liberally?

Conservation, not consumption, should be a goal. However, we're all going to consume. Being conscientious doesn't have to mean practicing ascetic self-denial. A progressive life should be abundant with meals, adventures, and everyday joys. Let's ensure that we spend in communitarian, socially conscious, green, creative, diverse ways . . . and that will be Spending Liberally.

## Buying Liberally: Purchase Politics

You've heard of "purchasing power," right? They call it power for a reason. Where you spend your money symbolizes what you're investing in. Businesses will compete for those dollars, even if it means they have to become better businesses. You don't even need to appeal to their better angels, if their lesser angels can get the job done.

Think about where you spend your money each month: clothing and transportation, electric bills and your cell phone, gifts and games, nightlife and necessities. What if every time you spent money, you also created social capital?

Stores get that you have an incredible amount of freedom in where and how you spend, which is why they spend so much time creating incentive programs such as frequent shopper cards. Credit cards also offer you points or miles or rebates because they get power from your purchases.

It would be terrific if you accrued karma points the way you collect credit card points. While there may not be a formal program (yet) for such a system, there are ways you can spend that will give and get more than just a commercial exchange.

**The Mom-and-Pop vs. The Big Box.** There are words for businesses that swoop into communities, undercut local businesses, shut out the competition, then jack up prices, limit selection, and undervalue workers. Pirates? Monopolies?

Big box stores.

I understand the appeal of the big box store: they can be convenient. Everything in one place. They offer low prices.

But what's the real cost of this abundance? It's not factored into the price, which is why the consumer is spared thinking about it. There are costs to the environment in the footprints of these mega-chains. There are costs to the workforce, small businesses, and the community. Big box stores put local stores out of business, reduce jobs, and devastate downtowns. When one big box store replaces dozens of smaller establishments, there's no incentive for employers to compete for labor; workers just accept what they can get: often minimum wage jobs, rarely with benefits.

The most famous culprit is Walmart. Walmart regularly promoted men over women. Walmart has a record of locking overnight workers in the store. Walmart has long fought any unionization effort. At one point, it was documented that Walmart's human resources department was helping full-time workers apply for food stamps because they did not earn enough to support their families.

Walmart, and other large scale chains, are capable of positive impact. When they agree to stock energy-efficient products, they boost the industry that produces them; and when they switch to more sustainable practices, that has a big impact across their chain. Walmart is the country's largest food retailer, so they have the ability to transform the market. They are also a company deeply invested in efficiency, as it affects their bottom line. The result is that they have instituted policies demanding less packaging for their items, and this has caused many manufacturers to reduce their waste. See, even Walmart can learn to spend liberally.

Some people have no choice but to shop at Walmart. There are ways to shop consciously within a big box, and the suggestions throughout this chapter about intentional purchasing can be applied anywhere.

411 First and foremost, though, if you have the opportunity, shop at the mom-and-pop stores.

They are the stabilizing staples of a community, the establishments where it's in the business's interest to know customers by name and keep employees in real jobs over time. They are more responsive to customer concerns and invested in community projects. A range of small stores employs more people at better wages than a single large store, creates more middle-class jobs, and supports stable families . . . who keep investing their money into the communities as well.

These neighborhood establishments add texture to your life. People are shaped by the memories they have from their local shops. These stores are where many of us learned lessons about trust and social interaction.

412 **Buy union.** If you want your money to support overall prosperity, make a point of spending on products that carry the union bug. By doing so, you support institutions that continue to raise working conditions across the country. You can be sure that the workers are benefiting from the purchase: paid a living wage,

given benefits for their families, and working in conditions that meet ethical and environmental standards.

If you don't buy strictly from union shops, you can ask where your products are made. You've heard about sweatshops, and there's a reason our country is proud that our history includes replacing sweatshops with decent jobs. Yet sweatshops exist around the world where workers are paid pennies, where their days are long and they are given no breaks, where they have no rights to complain and no job guarantees, and are discarded when they can't work anymore. In many sweatshops, child labor continues to be part of the workforce.

There are other brands in America that may not be union, but are sweatshop free, or guarantee (and publicize) their workers' wages and conditions. Once, it might have been hard to get this information. Now, there are resources all over the internet that make it easy. Surf through the "Green Pages" for a search engine to businesses that take their environmental impact seriously, or visit "The Responsible Shopper" to view the profiles of companies you might patronize.

**Be a conscientious customer—**Whatever your purchases, through your actions and questions push businesses to be better:

a. Learn the conditions of the workers that produced your purchase.

b. Check on the environmental record of a business.

c. Check on the politics of the business. Do they lobby? Do they donate to political causes?

d. Ask friends for recommendations and offer your own.

e. Choose items with less packaging.

**f.** Get a sense of the work environment in the store.

**g.** If an item is disposable, choose one that is recyclable or biodegradable.

**h.** Support independent producers and crafts-people.

**i.** Give feedback (praise *and* flack).

**j.** Ask yourself: Do I really need this?

In addition to acting individually, you always get more bang for your liberal buck when you act together. That's one thing the big box stores have right: by amassing a significant share of a market, they can move that market. That's true for you and your fellow shoppers.

There are many examples of collective consumerism that have allowed progressive purchasing power to flourish.

**Boycott.** If you don't like the practices of a particular business, stop shopping there. Make sure to tell the owner why, and make sure to take a lot of friends away from the business with you.

**Buycott.** Why only oppose what we're against? Let's also reward good behavior. Denying dollars may hurt a business, but collective spending can help one you like. The Buycott is a push to encourage people to spend their dollars on businesses making the right decisions.

**Create new markets.** Many people now get the opportunity on their energy bill to check off if they'd prefer their electricity come from alternative sources of energy. Eventually, enough people will make this choice, and there will be even more investment in those sources of energy. Organize people to demand something of a business, and build that incentive for the business. As more people purchase hybrid cars, the market for repairing and outfitting those cars will grow.

**Create alternatives.** If you can't get a business to behave the way you want, can you work around it? If what you want isn't sold in your local businesses, could it be created through collective creativity and ingenuity?

One company that decided to be an alternative and provides a model of living liberally is Working Assets. A San Francisco business, it's a do-gooder save-the-planet enterprise disguised as a series of for-profit ventures, most notably the CREDO Mobile phone company. I worked with Working Assets/CREDO a few years ago, and saw firsthand how they work and play liberally. But I wasn't just an employee; I'm also a member—a proud subscriber to CREDO cell service, and carrier of the Working Assets credit card.

The founders of Working Assets recognized a problem in the progressive movement. Nonprofits and political organizations were always scrounging for money. They didn't possess a reliable, respectable revenue stream to conduct their work. The creators of Working Assets saw a solution: progressives had plenty of funds they spent regularly on services like their telephone. Was there a way to funnel that money, which people willingly and regularly paid, through the progressive movement?

Working Assets got into the long-distance business, an area where people didn't feel great loyalty to their provider so would switch to an equivalent service if given a reason, such as a good cause and some coupons for free Ben & Jerry's ice cream. The company invested a portion of every phone bill into a pot of money that went to progressive nonprofit causes. Working Assets expanded into cellular service with CREDO Mobile.

If you're going to send your money some direction, you might as well give it to a company that:

**Donates profits.** A very transparent process pools money from the phone bills paid year-round and dedicates it to fifty national progressive nonprofits, across sectors like human rights and the environment. Members (the customers) nominate causes and vote for where their money goes.

**Respects its customers.** Working Assets is in constant communication with customers about both their service and their politics, inviting members to be partners in business and activism.

**Treats workers with respect.** CREDO employees have the ability to offer creativity and feedback, dress as they like, and enjoy kitchen facilities and common areas.

**Embodies ethical practices.** CREDO invests in environmental improvements in their office. They print phone bills on recycled paper and offer electronic alternatives. They are fair and proactive with customers (I've been late more than a few times) and they communicate about major decisions with their community. They also didn't help the Bush administration's illegal domestic spying program, unlike other major phone companies.

**Markets less.** A large cost of doing business in America is marketing, which drives up the price of products, and drives us crazy with an ad-infused culture. CREDO has much narrower, targeted outreach, relying on partners, word of mouth, and awareness among progressives.

**Lobbies for the public good.** Most telecommunications companies take stances to consolidate power and monopolize the market. In particular, Verizon and AT&T back efforts to create tiers of internet service to justify charging people for faster access to different websites. Working Assets could benefit from moves that hurt the public, but they put consumer rights first.

438

**Takes action.** CREDO invests money in progressive infrastructure, not only through donations but also supporting innovation and building tools and web applications the movement needs. They created a widget that allowed any website to become a hub of voter registration. They funded nonpartisan get-out-the-vote efforts. They support blogging and independent journalism. They run an activist e-mail list with which they rally for health care and energy reform and against war and cronyism.

439

They also find creative ways to do this activism with their actual phones. They've invested in text technology, and will text action alerts that call upon their customers to use their phones to call Congress. On Election Day, they gave everyone free outbound calls to encourage us to contact voters. They don't just want you to Spend Liberally by subscribing to them. They want you to Call Liberally as well.

I became a customer of their phone service in December 2006. More than three years later, my phone still works. I can't complain about that.

Working Assets obviously isn't the only company that lives its values. There are plenty of businesses working to earn our trust and improve our planet. Here are just a few that offer you alternatives:

**440** **Better World Club.** An alternative to AAA, which has a history of lobbying against public transit and promotes a car-crazed culture. Gives you the automotive support you need without sacrificing your politics. As they say: improve your car-ma.

**441** **Organic Valley.** A collective of family farmers that created a big enough business model to reach wider distribution than any individual farmer could achieve.

**442** **3R Living.** A provider of environmentally friendly gifts and household items, such as a backpack with solar panels that charges your computer or phone as you go about your day.

**443** **Etsy.** A website that allows independent artists and craftspeople to reach a far wider audience and allows buyers to support local creators.

**444** **Progressive Book Club.** A bookseller that features progressive authors and publishers and builds up a base of members so left-leaning voices get wider circulation and are pushed into the public discourse.

## Beware vs. Buy Now

Wherever you shop, there are a few easy guides that provide a green light or red light for your purchases.

**Beware: Plastic.** We're all going to own plastic items in our lives, but that's all the more reason to think twice before you purchase it. It feeds our petroleum-based economy, and it doesn't go away.

445

**Buy now: Used goods.** If you can find what you need secondhand, you help reduce the carbon footprint of your consumerism.

446

**Beware: Made in China.** Yes, the Chinese need to work, too—but their government doesn't do a whole lot to protect its workers or the world we all live in.

447

**Buy now: Local, handmade.** Get to know the people behind the product.

448

**Beware: Unaccountability.** If the store clerk can't tell you where an item is from, who produced it, or who takes responsibility for it, you may want to think twice.

449

**Buy Now: Anything from a lemonade stand.** Because it's always nice to support kids.

450

## Eating Liberally

As much as you reduce your purchases, you will still need to eat. Every day, you have three opportunities to "vote with your fork." Making a few relatively simple improvements to your diet can put your politics on your plate.

Until recently, this idea was pretty foreign to me.

I was a "growing boy" through my teenage years. That is, I ate ceaselessly. I loved all-you-can-eat buffets. I loved the endless meals in my college dining hall. I cared more about how big the portions were than what I was consuming.

Then *Fast Food Nation* opened my eyes to a wider view about the connections between what I ate and its impact on the larger world. Eric Schlosser's tremendous work details the detrimental impact the fast food industry has on public health, labor, and the environment and the industry's masterful manipulation of marketing, addiction, and market forces. The book made me question how my own eating habits related to those issues. I used to regularly purchase from McDonald's magical ninety-nine-cent menu. Since reading *Fast Food Nation*, I've completely cut fast food burgers from my diet.

Overall, I was not yet a food advocate when friends suggested Drinking Liberally needed to branch out. Kerry Trueman and Matt Rosenberg were avid blog readers and frustrated liberals. They suggested Eating Liberally, so they wouldn't have to talk politics on an empty stomach. Eating Liberally hosts gatherings about politics over food and about the politics *of* food.

---

## A Glossary on Gustatory Goodness

Loads of labels are attached to the food you eat. How do you know what you're spending your limited liberal dollars on? Look for:

★ **Organic.** Describes more natural approaches to farming, which is not reliant on chemical support, especially pesticides.

★ **Locally grown.** Food that comes from nearby sources, appealing to people who wish to reduce environmental impact of shipping food, avoid big agribusiness, and know more about their sources of food. Locavores believe that fresher local food is also healthier and tastier.

453

★ **Grass-fed.** Attributed to meat or products from animals that are raised on pasture, rather than grain, which is usually associated with mass production and adverse ecological impact.

454

★ **Fair Trade.** An approach to purchasing ingredients directly from farmers who often work together in co-ops and reinvest funds in their communities.

455

★ **Biodynamic.** A farming technique that works to find more balance in the use of the farmland, seeing the soil, animals, and produce as part of a unified ecosystem.

456

★ **Retrovore.** One who favors conservation over consumption. One who forages for food that's fresh, local, minimally processed, and grown with care. One who aspires to live in harmony with nature rather than pummel it into submission.

457

There is a large, diverse, passionate, informed, activist community engaged in every niche of food policy. Sadly, they too infrequently overlap with activists engaged in progressive electoral politics or more conventional issue advocacy. Many "foodies" see politics as messy, and few politicians speak to their issues meaningfully. Many progressive politicos place food in a personal sphere and ignore how much political decision-making goes into what we eat. That divide is slowly changing. Popular authors like Marion Nestle, Michael Pollan, and Eric Schlosser and films like *Food, Inc.* are promoting food issues in a new light. An increasing number of bloggers straddle the food movement and progressive organizing. They two communities are collaborating around farm subsidies, school lunches, and the drive to include food issues in public health, energy, and sustainability policies.

The politics of food is substantial; just as important, the food can be delicious. Many of us mistakenly assume that eating smartly may mean eating blandly. Eating Liberally proves you could eat well and eat good.

You don't need to be a food expert, or become consumed about what you consume, to make a few small changes that lead to much smarter choices.

---

## Six Steps to Start Eating Liberally

by guest contributor Kerry Trueman, cofounder of Eating Liberally

1. **Eat less meat.** Livestock production is a significant source of greenhouse gas emissions. Think of plant-based foods—beans, grains, fruits, veggies, nuts—as your own personal source of solar power.

2. **Cut back on industrially produced eggs and dairy.** All factory-farmed foods rely heavily on fos-

sil fuels. Opt for grass-fed animal products whenever possible.

3. **Support your local food producers.** They're your best source for sustainably grown foods, whether or not they're officially certified "organic." Save your "food miles" to splurge on things that don't grow in your region: spices, coffee, or chocolate (Fair Trade, of course!). `460`

4. **Limit your consumption of processed convenience foods,** which create tons of excess packaging and don't do your body (or soul) any favors. `461`

5. **Reduce food waste** by buying only what you're really going to eat. A whopping 40 percent of the food we produce goes to waste, generating massive amounts of methane. Convert your kitchen scraps to black gold by composting them yourself or taking them to a composting facility in your community. `462` `463`

6. **Take the time to make a meal from scratch** now and then, or grow even just a little of your own food. It will reconnect you with the seasons and the pleasures of fresh, homemade meals. Not a born chef or gardener? Find some folks who are, and hang out with them! They'll be happy to share the weeding and the feeding with you. `464`

Living—or eating—like a liberal is never just about making politics personal, but about making personal politics public. When it comes to eating habits, start with *what* to buy. Next, think about *how* to buy. The "how" takes you from living sustainably, healthily, and intentionally to living liberally: spending and eating in a way that connects to a community.

**Buy Local.** In addition to the health and environmental reasons, there's a classic community reason to buy local. The local farmer and grocer are going to be more invested in your community, more responsive to neighborhood needs, and more interested in being a local partner over the long haul.

My mother remembers from her childhood in Brooklyn when her mother sent her to the butcher. Grandma instructed her: "Tell him you're Mrs. Karp's daughter . . . he'll give you a good cut."

Would the butcher really have given a substandard piece of meat to a stranger? Regardless, he knew Mrs. Karp. He would see her again. He knew she talked to other neighbors. He didn't want her to take her business elsewhere. Knowing each other's names established a relationship that was good for both of them.

Supporting local stores makes it more likely that they will support your local interests. They may stock particular items you request, donate to neighborhood charities, or promote election efforts and community events.

Buy local, and you are investing in your community.

**Shop at farmers' markets.** Once upon a time, people grew their own food, or purchased from neighboring farmers or from a local store supplied by area farmers. With mass distribution, we began to patronize larger stores with more options, and consequently we had less sense of who produced the food we ate. Bigger and bigger companies got into the business of mass-producing food to supply the bigger and bigger stores. Eventually, fewer family farms could compete.

The wave of the future is sometimes a return to the past. Farmers' markets connect consumers directly to the producers again. They give local and independent farmers a chance and give consumers fresher produce and a stronger connection to their food.

**Join CSAs/farm-shares.** If you like farmers' markets, take the next step. Community-supported agriculture (or CSA) is a collective way of supporting local farms in return for consistent, reliable produce. Members pay a fixed fee for a season, guaranteeing farmers a reliable income. Members receive a weekly harvest. The exchange is made more affordable because of how many members are involved, demonstrating that a little teamwork goes a long way.

467

**Join a food co-op.** Supermarkets often have national or regional deals with food distributors. Thus, their shelves may be full of products that offend your politics, and their management may not be as interested in diversifying its offerings. In many cities, food co-ops offer an alternative. Co-ops specialize in purchasing from independent producers and distributors, often stocking healthier, more lifestyle-conscious items. They stock in bulk to serve the cooperative membership, which drives the price down from what you might find at a specialty store.

468

Many co-ops also expect members to work shifts. You may not be part of a farm or a community garden, yet you can contribute your labor to improving your food selection.

**Push your supermarkets.** Not every town has a food cooperative or farmers' market. You rely on A&P or ShopRite to provide

469

for you. They work on a large scale, and many of their partners are big industry producers. There's very little way to avoid that. What can you do?

You can organize. Ask supermarket managers to make local arrangements with area farmers and producers. Suggest items you would like the store to stock. Prove to them that there would be a market for your requests by asking neighbors to sign letters. These supermarkets may not be as concerned about community opinion, but they care about their bottom lines. If they know you'll buy, they'd be foolish not to sell.

Also, show them the success of Wegmans, New Seasons, Whole Foods, Trader Joe's, and other establishments that successfully market more green-conscious food options. Whole Foods' premium prices may not work for all of us, but your supermarket can find affordable options to create healthy alternatives.

**Advocate for food access.** In many urban areas, there are more McDonald's than there are providers of fresh fruit. In sprawling exurbs, there may be large consolidated supermarkets with little access to farm produce, because so many independent farmers were pushed out of business. When that's the case, it's difficult to make change through your spending habits, because there are no options to spend differently. That's when you need to advocate.

Talk to your elected officials about public health and access to food. This issue is growing in visibility, and more local city governments are coming to understand it. They also realize the health costs of limited food access and the detrimental impact poor diet has on youth. Give them reason to engage in the issue. Encourage them to look to other areas that already subsidize green markets or have begun to map "community foodprints." That way everyone can Eat Liberally.

## Drinking More Liberally: Politics in Every Pint

As you eat well, wash it down by drinking well. Ask about what
you're imbibing, and you'll quench your thirst to drink your way
into a more liberal life.

Ask your bartender:

★ Who brewed this? A large company or an independent brewery?

★ What are their labor practices?

★ How do they account for their environmental
impact?

★ Do they confront the ills associated with alcohol?

★ What are their politics?

You may not hold every drink up to this level of scrutiny. However,
it is useful to know that there are breweries and distilleries that
reflect your values while they refresh your spirit. You don't want
a moral hangover following a binge of bad booze.

**Drink locally.** We all know the big names in brewing, including Anheuser-Busch and Coors. The alternative: microbrews. These independent breweries frequently have less negative impact on the environment, more connection to the communities in which they are based, and great-tasting beers. While they rarely have national reach, microbrews can be found in most cities.

Often, microbrews are examples of craft beer. This movement breaks away from brewing as a mass-market competition. Craft beers focus more on the art of brewing and the taste of their product, using traditional brewing methods that rely less on rice and corn.

Because there's no way any one independent brewery can compete with the incessant marketing for the "King of Beers" or the "Taste of the Rockies," many microbrews are working together. They see each other as collaborators more than rivals as they promote a vision of drinking locally.

**Toast labor.** Yuengling, the nation's oldest brewery, recently engaged in a public effort to break its union. Why would a beer that wants to appeal to the workingman try to crush the workingman? After the Yuengling news spread on Daily Kos, hundreds of comments expressed disbelief and regret, as many readers announced they'd stop drinking it.

I hadn't planned on boycotting Yuengling, but I find myself more frequently choosing alternatives. Over Labor Day weekend, my friends brought a case of Yuengling to our holiday barbecue. I must have looked stricken; they asked me if I were ill. I explained my dilemma: Though it is inappropriate to reject a gift, I could not stomach Yuengling on Labor Day. Once I explained it, my friends understood. I returned the beer to the liquor store, explained the reasons to the clerk, and traded up for tastier and more conscientious Magic Hat.

Yuengling is losing loyal drinkers, one liberal liver at a time.

**Drink green.** I had the chance to tour the Magic Hat Brewery with the founder and owner Alan Newman. He spoke extensively about how they used less energy and produced less waste than their competitors. It didn't surprise me: Magic Hat has a cool, liberal feel, and Alan was a cool, liberal guy. If anyone were going to make green brewing its modus operandi, it would be a quirky Vermont-based brand.

475 476

The real motivation was the bottom line. These were cost-saving measures. As a small brand, Magic Hat carefully watched their use of resources.

Another brewery that famously makes its energy policy part of its marketing is the New Belgium Brewery in Colorado. The makers of Fat Tire generate their electricity from wind energy. They use a renewable resource to brew a drink that renews many grateful drinkers each day.

477

**Maker's Mark** is a brown drink with a green spirit. The distillery of this bourbon has reduced its environmental impact and recycles the by-products of distillation. As a loyal drinker of that whiskey, I felt my heart warm when I learned this (and no, I hadn't just done a shot). Now I tell everyone they can drink Maker's with a clean and green conscience.

478

There are Fair Trade vodka brands that support their suppliers from indigenous communities with fair wages and community investment. Other booze companies support the arts, live music, and community radio.

Saving the world is in the self-interest of the liquor lover. Global warming has hurt hops production. We need a healthy planet to keep our pint glasses filled.

**Confront the ills of alcohol.** Most big companies give to charity. Magic Hat targets causes related to the abuse of alcohol. They donate to domestic violence shelters and invest in sex education, family planning, and contraception. The tobacco industry has always tried to deny any of the deleterious effects of smoking. It's commendable to see a business that acknowledges the potential dangers of its own product and engages the issue, rather than ignores it.

**Drink politically.** Coors beer is a national institution, a well-known brand, a ubiquitous option. It's also the source of wealth that has helped fund the right-wing movement for the past decades.

Several large families have underwritten much of the conservative infrastructure that has been waging a concerted effort against a progressive agenda, functional government, and the American way of life. They finance organizations that push the our court system to the right; create right-wing message machines, think tanks, and echo chambers; support young conservatives; and distort the role of social welfare and government programs.

Every Coors six-pack you buy helps fund that movement. If you want to drink your politics, go dry on Coors. Honestly, you won't be missing much.

Sadly, they're not alone in putting their politics before their potential customers.

Anheuser-Busch, now part of the international InBev, is the maker of Budweiser, Beck's, and many other brands. This company sits on the board of the United States Chamber of Commerce, an organization that outspokenly denies global warming. We should tell Bud: we like the King of Beers, but we love Mother Earth more, and ask them to take a stand against the Chamber. 482

As the health care battle heated up, a handful of liquor companies decided to become involved. Guinness, Johnnie Walker, Bacardi, Baileys, and others wrote to their customers to ask them to oppose health care reform due to a phantom threat of "luxury taxes."

These companies that can have harmful effects on people's health were working against making health care affordable. Furthermore, many people who work in nightlife as waiters, bartenders, bar backs, and bouncers are rarely provided with medical benefits. They are often part-time, hourly workers, earning a lower minimum wage. Yet their own industry lobbies against their interests.

You might want to send Guinness and Johnnie Walker, frequent favorites of mine, the way of Yuengling. With all these bad-faith brewers, I'd worry that soon I'd be completely dry but fortunately with the growth of craft beer, that there's no doubt I'll keep drinking liberally. 483

## Investing Liberally

You can earn liberally. You can spend liberally. Now, invest liberally.

Despite the stereotype of being "tax and spend liberals," we're more often "earn and invest liberals"—we create the stable societal structures that allow people to earn more for themselves, their businesses, and their families. We invest that wealth in an America that produces for everyone. We share the benefits of our prosperity and produce dividends for the future:

an educated next generation, old age with dignity, a habitable planet, and resources that stretch further because we share them consciously.

Saving money and establishing wealth is not the purview of conservatives alone. As with all aspects of life, we liberals do it a little differently.

484**Switch to a credit union.** You may break free of the Agricultural Industrial Complex and the grip of Big Telecom. What can we do about the Big Banks?

Few people actually like their banks. Once upon a time, people did. They had neighborhood banks. Kids got lessons in financial education by starting junior savings accounts. Loan officers knew their communities, and people were proud to pay back loans because they knew their bankers.

But the bank of my childhood was bought. Then it was bought again. It became Fleet, which became Bank of America, and somehow I went from a neighborhood bank to having an account at one of the biggest, most heartless financial monoliths in the country.

They change fee structures and charge exorbitant fines. They battle against unions. They overcompensate executives who take massive risks and bring our financial system to the brink of insolvency.

While I politically differ with Bank of America, it has always appeared easier to stay put. I did not see an obvious alternative.

Credit unions offer a way out. Much like the neighborhood banks of old, these are localized establishments that hold and protect your money. They invest their holdings and yield interest, but unlike Big Banks, they invest in their communities. Quite the opposite of "too big to fail," these are often "too small to notice." They rarely market themselves or put their names on ballpark marquees.

Credit unions are governed by cooperative principles. Their members participate in decision making and democratically decide how to invest their shared capital. Credit unions spend resources to educate their members, allies, and stakeholders.

Bank of America, Chase, Citi, and Wells Fargo donate to good causes and offer resources on financial literacy, but I know my personal experience with them has never felt cooperative, democratic, or community-invested.

**Visit the Credit Union Co-op,** a site that explains credit unions and helps you find your local options. Many have debit/credit cards, participate in ATM networks, and give you all the familiar comforts of banking. Plus, we've never had to bail them out.

485

**Take part in socially responsible investment.** If you're not just looking to save, but looking to invest, you don't have to hand your money to UBS and call it a day. Nor do you have to place your bets on Exxon Mobil.

486

Research socially responsible funds. These funds consider the labor and environmental standards of the companies they invest in. They track the community practices of their investments and publish reports on how these businesses behave. While you're not necessarily investing in "good" business, like solar power or microgrants, at least you will be certain that you are not investing in companies that do bad.

Keep in mind that this isn't always easy or obvious. Many companies may make improvements in one area, like environmental awareness, while falling short on human rights practices. This is where it becomes tricky for a liberal. Do you support only companies that have already achieved a high level of progressive credibility, or would you invest in a company that is in the process of improving but has not reached its socially responsible goals?

Furthermore, there are plenty of big companies that take part in "greenwashing." They showcase very specific environmental improvements, but are not transforming their practices. Even Exxon runs ads about saving the planet.

In the end, you'll need to do your own research and decide your own priorities. Check out the Social Investment Forum for studies on this type of investment, or look to a group like Social Funds that investigates many of the socially responsible investment vehicles available. Consider a firm like Domini, which has an explicit social aim in how it manages individual and institutional investments.

No need to rely on brokers. You can run your own investments. It can be daunting to research all the possibilities and track each business that interests you, so do what any good liberal does: do it with others. Start your own investment club.

This tried-and-true concept empowers people to try their hand at investment, pool knowledge, and tie their financial fates to those of friends and neighbors. The Tucson chapter of Drinking Liberally took it further, creating an Investing Liberally club. It makes sense: you share values with each other; now create value with one another as well.

**Be a conscious shareholder.** It's not enough in a democracy to vote, then wait four years to see how things play out. You need to remain involved to hold your elected officials accountable; they need to hear from you to know how they are doing, and you need to organize with other voters to threaten your representatives when they're not getting the job done.

We accept that notion with politics, but very few of us apply it to corporate governance. Many of us own stocks, yet few of us take seriously our rights and responsibilities as owners. We tend to look at our shareholder status as a bet. We let the people we're betting on make the decisions. Then we're surprised when the companies don't behave as sustainably, diversely, and intentionally as we'd like.

Think of the word: "shareholders." We are sharing something, and like any communitarian enterprise, it's only going to be as good as we all make it. We share responsibility, share decision making, and share the fortunes. So get involved.

Shareholder actions have increased in recent years so much that white-shoe law firms have been advising corporate boards on how to prepare for them. Why should they be scared of their shareholders? Well, shareholders often are the engine behind changing the management. They can also become the impetus for making a company behave better to the world around it.

There are several ways to become an active shareholder:

**Use those proxy votes.** If you own stock, you get voting power. That's the easiest place to start.

492

**Organize a shareholder resolution.** If you don't like what you're voting on, create new choices. Similar to organizing a workplace, this is a matter of finding other shareholders who share your concerns. Social Funds, which advocates for socially responsible investment, offers a clear guide on who can create a resolution and how to do it.

493

**494**   **Sell.** Personally divesting from a company, getting a group of shareholders to sell, or even causing an institutional investor to back away is a big decision. Is it better to remain involved in a company in order to change it? Or is there a time when you want to have nothing to do with it? You will need to decide for yourself where that line is drawn.

**495**
**496**   Use your shareholder power to ask about the distribution of wealth within the company. Ask how the business behaves in new communities. Ask for a plan to reduce the company's carbon footprint. Recruit others to ask with you if you want to get answers or, even better, shape solutions.
**497**
**498**

# CHAPTER 7
# ACTING
# LIBERALLY

> *What is conservatism?*
> *Is it not adherence to the old and tried,*
> *against the new and untried?*
> —ABRAHAM LINCOLN

> *I'm not a member of any organized*
> *political party, I'm a Democrat!*
> —WILL ROGERS

You rise and shine and start your day liberally. You're conscientious about what you buy and what you use, you greet your neighbors, lead by example with your family, engage your coworkers. You now think twice about the movies you go to and the sites you surf. You are already changing the world.

Now do more.

It's great to internalize liberal lessons in your everyday life, and even better to share that lifestyle with those around you. Real change, though, requires a step deeper into politics. Ultimately, we need to make systemic change, which comes from banding together around our ideals and electing representatives who will live up to our values. We need to push those in power and not only involve ourselves in the issues we face in

499
500

our neighborhoods but also get involved in the issues we face
as a society.

Drinking Liberally has been a gateway into this type of political activism for many. Our vision was that you would start by
becoming more aware and confident in your views by gathering
at the bar. Then your drinking buddy would convince you to
come make some phone calls for a campaign. Before you knew
it, your new social circle would lead you into the field on Election Day.

In 2004, a dozen of us rented a van and drove out to Pennsylvania
to knock on swing-state doors in an effort to prevent Bush's
second term. We spent four days together, culminating in a late
drive home on Tuesday, November 2nd. As we drove, the news
coming over the radio got worse and worse. We had spent four
days waking up early and staying up late. We had knocked on
doors in the cold and made more phone calls from the office at
night. We had lived on floors, traveled in a cramped vehicle, and
even wore matching shirts. We must have been best friends.

The funny thing: only a couple of us had even known each other
before the launch of Drinking Liberally. Most of us had become
friends over the six months prior to this election road trip. But
the strength of our bonds that formed through our weekly social
gatherings, galvanized by the intensity of a critical election, led
us from Drinking Liberally to Acting Liberally.

Taking action shouldn't be a chore separate from the tips listed
throughout this book. It should be an extension of your life and
integrated with the values of the liberal lifestyle: it should be
rooted in community, it should be an easy and accessible activity
that meets you where you are in life, it should be communal
and expressive, and, yes, it should even be fun.

Acting Liberally isn't something you do instead of going to the movies, creating community dinners, or improving your workplace with your colleagues. Your social networks give you the strength and resolve to look beyond your community and take action to reshape our government and our society.

Fortunately, great organizations are doing this work, threading social life with political action in ways that are enjoyable and politically potent. Maybe one of these examples will inspire you to Act Liberally . . . and maybe you will become an inspiration to others.

## Beating the Red State Blues: The Snake River Freedom Coalition

In 2006, several high school students in the conservative town of Idaho Falls decided to protest the war. Maybe they had read stories in the news and said enough was enough. Maybe they knew people who had been sent to Iraq. Maybe they were fearful, as teenagers would rightfully be, that perpetual war would bring back a draft.

They engaged in a creative protest. They wrote the word "WAR" under the word "STOP" on traffic signs around town, thus turning street corners into "STOP WAR" billboards.

Unfortunately, that's also vandalizing public property, and anything that interferes with traffic signs jeopardizes public safety. So they were arrested and punished for their actions. They were fined for the cost of replacing the signs and assigned community service hours. More than the penalties, they suffered as their conservative community ostracized them. They worried whether this would affect their ability to attend college.

The members of Idaho Falls Drinking Liberally followed the story and decided to take action. This club is more than a group of beer drinkers. As with many of our chapters in red towns in red states, the Liberal Drinkers become a tight-knit community. They lean on each other for political information and for moral support. In each other's company, they no longer feel isolated in their beliefs. In some areas, Drinking Liberally the only event that uses the word "liberal," and many chapters serve as organizing hubs for local progressive causes.

The Idaho Falls members have marched in the town's Fourth of July Parade as a Drinking Liberally cadre. They host community barbecues and guest speakers. They arrange political comedians and musicians to tour their conservative area. Talk about Putnam-style social capital: they helped paint one member's new home.

This group decided to act on behalf of the antiwar high school students. They began the Snake River Freedom Coalition, a new organization, and committed to three actions:

1) The group wanted to raise money to cover the youths' fines. They auctioned off the vandalized stop signs, which had become the possessions of the students, and made shirts and stickers with the STOP WAR image.

2) The Coalition joined the teens for their community service. The teens were no longer alone. Instead of feeling isolated and ashamed, they now had the support of others literally standing by their side.

Additionally, it turned community service from a punishment into a public good. This action sent a different message about community involvement and made the teens feel less criminalized by their punishment.

**3)** The Coalition wanted to ensure that high schoolers could express their opposition to the war legally. Protest should not have to destroy public property or jeopardize college applications. The group began working with high school peace activists, supporting their efforts to engage in creative, effective, and safe protest. `507`

What began as a way for a community of social peers to take action has grown into a community of its own. The Snake River Freedom Coalition now hosts the Loving Day celebration, marking the Supreme Court decision to strike down laws against interracial marriage. Last year they honored local organizers, labor leaders, and businesses. They did so at an awards dinner: a potluck barbecue at their local park. `508`

## Party Politics

While Drinking Liberally was promoting political involvement one pint at a time in New York City, a kindred spirit was hitting the road on the West Coast. The Oregon Bus Project worked to engage young people in political action in fun, social ways. They created actions around education, the environment, health care, and the economy. And they had a bus.

The bus became a physical manifestation of the liberal spirit: people who were part of a movement together were able to move together. The bus would make a social event out of a day of canvassing, driving forty people on an adventure. It was a field trip for politics. `509`

They hosted events like Candidates Gone Wild, a night that brought local candidates to speak to packed houses of young voters. Rather than creating a night of stump speeches and stiff forums, the Bus Project engaged the candidates in talent show/talk show style events that loosened up the politicians and opened up politics for new audiences. In New York, our

version was Mayoroke—any candidate in the 2005 municipal race could stump . . . but first they had to sing.

The Bus Project will best be known for Trick or Vote. What do you need to do to get people to vote? You talk on them. You knock on their doors. What day do people willingly open their doors to strangers? Halloween. It only took two centuries of American elections for some folks in Portland, Oregon, to figure out that Halloween always falls within a week or so of Election Day.

Young progressives, attired in costumes that range from the politically satirical to the straight-up ridiculous, hit the streets, a couple feet taller than most trick-or-treaters, and with a taller order: engage people in politics and remind them to vote.

This activity is spreading across the country. It's localized, it's social, it's fun; it allows you to take a holiday and invest it with more meaning; it creates a shared experience for the activists and the residents and builds on an existing shared occasion. And it's goofy. People don't get annoyed. They take notice, which means it is effective. At the end of a night of Trick or Vote you will have spoken to more people than on your usual canvass.

In Durham, North Carolina, good works are mixed with good vibes by another group of "Tractivists." They're part of Traction, which spices up politics and brings younger North Carolinians into progressive action—through kickball, movies, bike rides, and art openings. This is not your usual political fare.

Much like Drinking Liberally, Traction is a gateway. They host purely social events to draw you in. They create other events that mix social and political impulses. Then they organize outings that are particularly activist. On cold weekends before Election Day, they throw field day parties, which draw people out for games and chili and use the opportunity to energize them to vote. They invite you out to pick blueberries, then teach you to become advocates for local agriculture. They bring you on a bike ride and end up engaging you about the area's green spaces.

Other groups put the party into politics on Election Day. People always wonder how to turn out voters in low-turnout areas: knock on more doors? Send more fliers? What if you invite the community out to a party?

From this notion, Party at the Polls was born. These parties take place near polling sites on Election Day and are nonpartisan and open to the public. They don't require you to vote in order to get your burger. Rather they made it convenient, desirable, and community-oriented to come out and vote. Local businesses donate food and drink, performers and community leaders come speak, and local radio helps promote.

Researchers at Yale University demonstrated that it worked. Per dollar spent on nonpartisan get-out-the-vote activities, inviting neighbors to a community party or barbecue near the polling site turned out more voters than any other investment of the same resources. In 2006, Working Assets promoted these Parties at the Polls in conjunction with partners like the League of Young Voters, Young People For, and Democracy Matters. Each election, new organizations continue to employ this idea.

You have to connect to people in ways that work with their lives. Not everyone is ready to step beyond his or her comfort zone. If you can create a community impulse to vote, you're strengthening democracy and strengthening your community.

We should reinforce positive political habits by associating political involvement with fun activities. If "participation" means standing in line in a school cafeteria to vote, it's not going to bring a smile to your face. What if you associated political participation with music? HeadCount brings issue advocacy messaging and voter registration to concerts. Politics becomes part of a hip experience.

What if you created a memory that connected politics and baseball? Baseball is America's pastime, and ballparks love to swell with shows of patriotic pride. It makes you love your country, love your team, . . . and love your vote? That's in part what inspired Get In The Game, a nonprofit that registers voters at baseball games and other sporting events around the country.

My sister started this organization in the summer of 2004. After Major League Baseball said that nonpartisan voter registration was "too political" for a league-wide partnership, Arielle contacted each team for permission to register voters at their stadiums. The Yankees were the first team to sign on. The Yankees may not always be good neighbors, but they know good PR when they see it.

Arielle is a die-hard Democrat and even more die-hard Yankee fan. However, she puts both loyalties away when she puts on her nonpartisan Get In The Game T-shirt. She has registered Republicans . . . and even Red Sox Fans. Hey, everyone deserves a vote.

## Making the Call

A feature of every political campaign is phone-banking. You call potential voters to identify their leanings, persuade them, or remind them to vote. Volunteers gather in large rooms with dozens of phone lines. Smart volunteer coordinators order pizza to give the event a social feel. Usually the gatherings are in big offices—at union halls or law firms—and the scene is not particularly fun.

In 2004, organizers realized that technology could free campaigns from the staid office environment. We had cell phones. Many of us had more nighttime and weekend minutes than we knew what to do with. Why not burn those minutes calling voters?

Democracy in the Park innovated a new vision for phone banks: come out to Central Park on a weekend afternoon, lounge on a picnic blanket, snack, laugh, and call voters. Soon, there was Democracy in the Quad, a college expansion that encouraged students to organize in their campus commons. [519]

Two years later, in the 2006 election, MoveOn had developed the tools to allow people all across the country to organize house parties around swing-state calls. MoveOn would give you access to the call lists online and track the calls you and other volunteers were making at countless events. When you come to someone's home, you feel more connected to the host and other volunteers than you might at a phone bank in an office. Those calling parties have led people to join other group actions such as letter-writing campaigns and rallies. They also introduce volunteers to new political friends with whom they go the movies or out for a drink. These house parties made a political act into a community act. [520]

# Old School

Twenty-somethings in and around 2004 did not reinvent politics. While a young generation brought fresh energy and new technology to the political landscape, making socializing part of politics is the tried-and-true approach of the Democratic Club. At their core, these clubs were all about getting votes. Club leaders could deliver votes on Election Day, which made them influential in electing public offices and party positions.

However, these clubs weren't simply lists of voters and groups of reliable volunteers. Year-round activities made the clubs a center of community life that kept members involved beyond Election Day. The activities were more than political. The clubs were more than debate societies. They were active in the whole lives of their members: where they lived and worked, their fortunes and misfortunes.

The best existing model of this old school club is the McManus Democratic Association, which for over a century has held sway in the Democratic Party on the west side of Manhattan. The club was founded by Thomas "The" McManus in the 1890s when he defeated famed Tammany Hall ward-heeler George Washington Plunkitt in the race for district rep. McManus had no intention of overturning the power structure. He just wanted his piece of it. His club became an independent piece of the Tammany machine. For the next eleven decades, as sons and nephews took on his role, a man named McManus has been the district leader of Hell's Kitchen. As Tammany lost power and the subsequent generations of power brokers emerged, McManus endured.

How'd they pull off surviving the sea change in city politics? They acted as more than a political force. The McManus Club was always first to welcome immigrants to the neighborhood. Without question, they tapped into this new bloc of voters by registering them to vote, teaching them to use voting machines, and telling them who to vote for. They really cultivated loyalty by doing more: they helped all members, including immigrants, find apartments and jobs; they arranged legal advice when necessary; and consoled community members when they lost loved ones.

As Reformers replaced old-school Democrats in neighborhood after neighborhood throughout New York, the new clubs focused on organizing endorsement meetings and circulating petitions to add candidates to ballots. The McManus Club still hosts office hours with volunteer lawyers two nights a week. They still make calls for people behind on their rent. They attend community board meetings to speak for local establishments. They realized that to be successful in the political business, you should be in the community business.

Jim McManus is the current district leader, a post he's held for forty years. He throws a birthday party every year on the Sunday before the Democratic primary. You celebrate Jim, eat free sandwiches and drink cold beers, see your neighbors, share long tables in a large church basement . . . and you get introduced to the candidates you're expected to vote for two days later. Traction and Party at the Polls have nothing on these guys.

While the McManus office may be decorated with artifacts dating back decades, and many of their regular members are well into their senior years, this club is more than a holdover from the past. It has remained politically relevant because it has changed with its community. A century ago, it was a club of Irish immigrants; now Columbian and South Asian immigrants are part of the membership. The McManus Club did not find its strength in a particular culture or ethnicity. It has adjusted to include whoever makes up the cultural landscape of New York.

The Club is also open to new politics. In 2003, as the Democratic presidential primary heated up, the newly formed Drinking Liberally wanted to watch the debates together. The McManus Club opened its doors to us, bought us beers, and made us feel right at home. Jim was delighted to have a crew of twenty-somethings in the old building, hearing old stories and bringing new life to the club. Over the years, the Club has consistently welcomed new political groups to use their space.

The McManus Club's crowning annual event is a St. Patrick's Day Breakfast. More than 500 people crowd a T.G.I. Friday's before the St. Pat's parade. Every local politician shows up. The party begins at 7 AM. The senior citizens from the Club start lining up at 6:30 AM outside the restaurant. I was not invested in St. Patrick's Day before I first attended the breakfast. Now I would not dream of missing it. It is clearly a political event, but without stump speeches, debates, or petitions. It is nothing more than people sharing drinks and food and finding cause to be together. That's politics enough.

I've attended one event that has rivaled the McManus St. Patrick's Day breakfast as the epitome of social politics: the Tom Harkin Steak Fry. The long-serving Iowa senator knows his crowd. They want to support him, and they like a good party. Senator Harkin he throws a field day—a regional festival with vendors and booths, a grandstand stage, and 15,000 people in a balloon field in Indianola.

At the 2006 Steak Fry, then–freshman senator Barack Obama's speech fueled speculation about his presidential ambitions. In 2007, all the Democratic candidates attended and took turns addressing the first-in-the-nation caucus-goers. Everyone watched as though listening to an outdoor music festival: leaning back on lawn chairs and picnic blankets, eating meat and corn from Styrofoam plates, and drinking cheap beer.

It was Drinking Liberally on steroids.

This is more than a social outing. It is a major fundraiser for the senator. Your fee to join the party is a donation to his reelection effort. He has become such an institution that supporting him politically feels like a donation to your community. Every contribution is a way of taking action. Every small donation gives politicians the financial and moral boost to push ahead. You might have thought you were hitting a field day, but in fact you were Giving Liberally. Which counts as Acting Liberally.

## Activism 101

Not all action needs to be a party. Political involvement can take the form of working with disenfranchised communities and learning the challenges others face in their lives. It can be the tedious act of testifying at City Council, where you might wait hours for your five minutes at the podium. Your political participation may cause doors to be slammed in your face, and as you get closer to November, the rain gets icier.

525

526

When you engage liberally with a social spirit and act as a community, those difficulties become manageable. You share the frustration with your friends, who have experienced the same, and soon it becomes a common bond or a mark of honor, rather than a source of weariness. You grab a drink after a day in the field and replenish your commitment to the cause. You see the change in the community in which you work and

### What if you were Acting Conservatively?

You'd be part of a campaign that traded on fear and division, that wanted to dial back progress and ignore the course of history, and you'd probably end up ashamed of what the people around you were up to: like attacking abortion doctors or screaming that our president was born in Kenya.

witness the results of your efforts. There are just three tricks to any good activism: make it easy, make it social, make it rewarding.

**527** **Make it easy.** The challenges will not be easy to overcome. The work itself will not be painless. But it should be simple for people to get involved.

**528** **Organize it for the volunteers.** Don't make newcomers do a lot of guesswork about the task. Be clear about when and where to show up and what to expect there. Arrange car pools, sign folks up in advance, and follow up to confirm.

**529** **Bring it to the volunteers.** Could the project be done close to home? Could people participate in their natural habitat: a home, park, or café? When volunteers can engage in their familiar settings, it becomes easier for them and reaffirms that politics can fit into your life.

**530** **Remember to translate!** Entering a situation and not knowing the jargon is frustrating and isolating. Don't assume that everyone knows the terms of the trade, or even that they are as familiar with all the issues. Provide a primer, a basic introduction to each activity. When everyone has the same tools and terms, you will have a stronger team.

**531** **Make it social.** When you do an action together, you have the joy of common purpose, and you become involved more deeply. Acting liberally gives you the chance to learn from each other and support each other.

**532** **Make it easy to invite friends.** Ask people if they'd like to bring a buddy. Make it easy for them to do so. Your volunteer might feel more confident, you get an extra participant, and you start the project with a social rapport.

**Keep it casual.** Even if you have a lot of work to do, make sure people know they can chat and laugh. Introduce everyone at the start. They'll be sharing an experience—empower them to have a dialogue about it by knowing who else is with them. Make sure folks take breaks to keep their spirits up.

533

**Host an after party.** Every good action should have a social event after it. This may be a chance to decompress and debrief. It could be an opportunity to connect with others who didn't participate in the action and for them to see what they missed. It's a way to recharge your batteries and strengthen your community. If people have a beer when the day is done, they're more likely to come back again, because they will have bonded with other folks as well.

534

**Make it rewarding.** There are frequent occasions when volunteering can feel fruitless. You don't see results, or see the bigger picture. I remember being asked by volunteers once why they were calling voters and not persuading them. They were told just to ask questions about preferences but not to offer more information or engage in conversation. It was my first campaign, and I didn't know why. It turns out that campaigns have phases. In some phases you just identify whether voters are likely to support your candidate. You do this so in later phases you can target the voters that support you and not waste limited time calling the voters who don't. The bigger picture makes sense. However, if nobody explains the strategy, you'll feel like you're wasting your time. From the perspective of the campaign staff, it may seem like a burden to explain the strategy, but it always pays off if it keeps people involved.

535

**Lay out the big picture.** People will often do very minute tasks if they see how it fits into a grand scheme. Laying out the road map keeps people from feeling like they're just engaged in busywork.

**Mark progress and celebrate victories.** Talk to people about what they've accomplished. Demonstrate how their role contributes to a pattern of real change. One of the most inspiring moments I've experienced was in New Hampshire in the fall of 2008. We were heading out to knock on doors and we knew many people would not be home or would refuse to talk to us. The volunteer coordinator reminded us that in 2000, Al Gore had lost New Hampshire by a few thousand votes. There were a few thousand of us going into the field that day. If each of us connected with three voters, that would be the margin that would have changed the course of America. That got us motivated.

Many campaigns forget to celebrate their accomplishments. The staff gets caught in the burden of the longer battle. For activists, it's important to note when progress has been made. It keeps people energized and engaged.

**Saying thank you.** Thank you to the hosts in every state around the country, and increasingly around the world, who decided they were proud of the word "liberal" and willing to mix their political and social lives, and volunteer to help others do so as well.

A toast to the tens of thousands of Liberal Drinkers who want to improve our world, promote a progressive agenda, and have decided to do so one pint at a time.

I raise a glass to all the folks that have steered, shaped, and led Living Liberally: co-founder of the original DL, Matt O'Neill; our partner, Katrina Baker; David Alpert, who saw something much larger in this little club; Katie Halper, who kicked off the first Laughing Liberally; Wendy Cohen and Leigh Wolinsky who envisioned Screening Liberally; Kerry Trueman and Matt Rosenberg who cooked up Eating Liberally; our fellow national leaders in New York: Greg Rae, Claire Silberman, and Mary Bruch; and our leadership team, past and present, around the country: Adam Bartel of Cincinnati, Chris Blazejewski of Providence, Mark Campbell of Charlotte, Cass Chulick of Spartanburg, Amy Clinton of Winston-Salem, Heather Culligan of Salt Lake City, John Erhardt of Denver, Susan Harrison of San Francisco, Dan Henry of Idaho Falls, Tom Holland of Oklahoma City, Amie Hollis of Nashville, Greg Leding of Fayetteville, Robin Marty of Minneapolis, John McClelland of Addison, Bill Nothstine of Portland, Bill Poorman of Peoria, Amanda Mittlestadt Riordan of Des Moines, Jeremiah Roth of Salt Lake City, Jesse Rubin of San Diego, Vicki Sansbury of Louisville, McKay Schwalbach, Marcus Williams of Charlotte. And of course to Josh Bolotsky, our National Program Coordinator of three years, who kept it all going and growing.

Three cheers to our organization's creative inspirations along the way: Owen Roth, who created the name; Daniel Greenfeld who gave us a logo; Johnny Dirt of Rudy's for opening his backyard; Danny DePamphilis of Rudy's for being the consummate host; Andrew Hoppin, the first person to export Drinking Liberally beyond New York City.

Special acknowledgment to guest contributors: Katie Halper, Josh Bolotsky, Franz Hartl, and Hayley Siegel. Many friends and fellow schemers contributed the ideas throughout the book, especially to the group project of developing the lists of literature, music, and other cultural offerings. In addition to the leaders and hosts listed before, these brainstormers include Fred Gooltz, Jen Johnson, Allison Kilkenny, Elana Levin, Dave Levy, Leah Plunkett, Bede Sheppard, Brian Sonenstein, Shaunna Thomas, Alex Urevick-Ackelsberg, Josh Wojcik; and Laughing Liberally regulars Lee Camp, Matthew Filipowicz, Jamie Kilstein, Negin Farsad, Baratunde Thurston who contributed ideas and humor. And thank you for the support and inspiration I've received from Governor Howard Dean, Markos Moulitsas, Matt Stoller, and the good people at CREDO, MoveOn, Music For America, ActBlue, Advomatic, Netroots Nation, Open Left, The Tank, and our many allies who are building political culture in our country.

The book itself would not have happened without Ann Treistman of Skyhorse Publishing insisting that there was, in fact, a book to be written. The book would not have been beautiful without designer Paul Pierson, who has offered his inspired talent to Living Liberally through the years. The book benefitted from the edits of Katrina, Matt, Kerry, Josh, Julie Hilimire, my father and sister, and of Anne Jump, whose understanding of how to support and steer an author helped me in ways I could not have improvised on my own.

Finally, of course, a toast to the liberals closest to me. One grandmother insisted until her final day that we donate to the ACLU; one grandmother showed me that everything I needed was walking distance from home; Casey Selzer, with whom I live liberally each day; my sister Arielle, who took time off the campaign trail to read and re-read every sentence; and my parents, Suzanne and Eric, who brought me to a Mondale rally when I was six years old.

**Cheers.**

# CONCLUSION

## A Day in Holland, Michigan

During the writing of this book, I went to Holland, Michigan, to officiate a friend's wedding. It was an intimate affair, mostly family. I was invited because the bride and groom had different religious backgrounds and they wanted a neutral officiant. I had been ordained by an organization that certifies laypeople to perform rites reserved, in many states, for the clergy.

I had never been to Holland, but I was warned that it was "very conservative." The groom alluded to it. Other friends laughed and cautioned me that it would be one of the most conservative towns I'd ever been to.

What would that look like. A dry town? Confederate flags? Angry anti-Obama signs in every window? Having spent most of my life in a liberal areas in central New Jersey, Cambridge, and New York City, I was a little nervous. The bride and groom lived in Chicago, but how would their families, from these conservative towns, react to a long-haired East Coast Jewish liberal arriving to marry their children?

When I got there, I found a small city with a tidy, walkable downtown. There were establishments for locals and for the college campus near the town's center. There were pocket parks and courtyards dotting the streets, with public benches every block down the main strip.

Maybe conservative towns aren't so bad.

There were churches everywhere as well, in a greater density than where I grew up. They were classic, stately buildings, with proud facades and well-manicured lawns. The churches even outnumbered the banks, which also embodied a municipal bravado with public fountains, tall doors, and strong brick frames.

Together, these banks, churches, downtown improvements, and open spaces created a heart of the town that felt very welcoming and communal. I could imagine these features encouraging inter-action with your neighbors and pride in your town identity.

Then I met the people.

The two families mingling around the nuptials were white, unpretentious, and had northern Midwestern accents. I was prepared to be viewed as an outsider, ready to tiptoe through a few political debates. So when, the bride and groom's parents and grandparents inquired about the nature of my ordination, I was hesitant, almost apologetic, in explaining what certified me for this affair.

I explained how the Church of Universal Life serves to democ-ratize the clergy. Then the bride's grandmother spoke up. "We have a gal who does that in Elk Rapids," she announced. "She does weddings and funerals, down by the bay." It became clear that the "gal" was in her sixties. Grandma thought it was great that people were taking ownership of their own services and inviting loved ones to play a role. She was curious how I had prepared, and was delighted to learn I had spoken with the happy couple about their relationship, their hopes and fears, the language and images that most reflected their feelings, and their future together.

"It's just wonderful that you take all that into consideration," she said. "The best weddings do. And I've seen a lot of weddings." That's when she revealed that for twenty-eight years, she'd worked at the local Catholic church, where she was a devoted parishioner.

This warm, welcoming woman who had set me completely at ease was the "religious" grandmother we had been concerned about upsetting with our unconventional service. Far from being upset, she was enthusiastic.

Far from being scrutinized, I felt embraced.

Later, I met the bride's grandfather, an old, slightly portly, kindly looking gentleman. Since he was the oldest white male there, I thought for sure he would be the more conservative voice. Instead he shared his wish that a poem he wrote about living in peace would be translated into all languages and brought to every country in the world. He also sang "Only You" a cappella for the newlyweds' first dance.

I wasn't debating with the man as I expected. I was singing along with him.

The groom's father told me about the excitement he had seen around the state for Obama. The groom's childhood friends, who still lived in the right-leaning upstate towns of their youth, told me how infuriating it was to combat the talking points of Fox News. The groom's brother-in-law, who ran a local auto dealership, talked with me about how the government program "cash for clunkers" was working for him.

He and his wife, the groom's sister, live in Holland. He said Holland was a place where people ask you what church you belong to as a way to get to know you. She said it was the kind of town where people ask her what her husband does rather than what she does. Yet they were both Holland residents and neither of them fit their own stereotypes of the town.

Despite warnings from East Coast friends and these Holland natives, I experienced a very different town. In my short time there, I found the locally brewed craft beer. I visited the hotel, which boasted of its LEED Certification for environmental sustainability. I saw signs of the regional farmers' market the town promoted. I walked past the independent cinema on Main Street advertising a season of socially conscious documentaries and art-house flicks.

I found the local independent coffee shop that served Fair Trade coffee, offered free Internet service, and charged you less if you used a reusable mug. With fliers for concerts plastered across its walls, snarky satire mags for free on its shelves, and a mix of alternative high school patrons and college kids with laptops propped open, it looked exactly like what you'd expect at the edge of a campus in a town of 30,000.

What made this surprising was that I'd internalized the idea that Holland would be a different world. And here I was, drinking from a big yellow mug (the place also has an honor policy if you're in a rush; you just drop money in a cup and go), feeling very much like I was among my people. I found a free monthly paper about sustainability in western Michigan, replete with condemnations of big box stores and Walmart's environmental practices. I found photocopied signs for Holland's ninth annual Tulipanes Latino Cultural Festival.

I found one pinup advertising "a church as liberal as Jesus." If you're going to be a liberal in a religious town, that's one way to do it.

The day after the wedding, I attended part of the Tulipanes Festival: a worship service in Centennial Park. The prayer service was fully bilingual. The youthful, rocking, God-loving musical medleys had verses in both English and Spanish.

Families of different ages and hues along with a good showing of senior citizens filled the lawn, and young kids sang and danced along. The sermon was on needing to accept change when we seek to build something strong together: a house, a community, a country.

Holland is not a liberal town. There are probably many people in that town who would express their fear of immigrants. There are also people prepared to embrace another culture. There are residents who complain about big government, high taxes, and Democrats wanting to take their guns away. Other residents want to make the town greener, increase public transportation, and support the arts.

Despite my presumptions—my prejudices—going in, I would not have known what typical Hollanders believed without talking to every one of them. Maybe there was no such person as a typical Hollander.

Even in that "conservative" town, there are liberals. Some broadcast it proudly, others hold their beliefs more quietly, and some find ways to meld liberal values with the town's more religious, traditional character. There are probably many Hollanders who would never use the word "liberal" to describe themselves and would be astonished by the characterization. Yet they were living freely, diversely, compassionately, and sustainably. They were living for one another, not for themselves alone.

From the publicly funded parks and community spaces to the embrace of multiculturalism, Holland is doing plenty to be proud of. That might not be left or right on the political spectrum. That might win praise from as many Republicans as Democrats.

In my view, it's just more evidence that in every corner of the country, Americans are living liberally.

# APPENDIX
# THE COMPLETE
# 538 WAYS
## TO LIVE WORK AND PLAY LIKE A
# LIBERAL
## CHECK THEM ALL OFF!

 Read this book

- [1] Drink liberally

- [2] Choose your morning news

- [3] Listen to public radio

- [4] Cover your television

- [5] Leave magazines out and open around your house

- [6] Choose local stations

- [7] Watch public television

- [8] Switch off Fox News in the mornings

| 9  | Read the morning paper or online news |
|----|----------------------------------------|
| 10 | Make your lunch |
| 11 | Use a reusable lunch bag |
| 12 | Compost |
| 13 | Know your recycling rules |
| 14 | Shut down your house when you're out |
| 15 | Turn off the AC or turn down the thermostat |
| 16 | Turn off lights |
| 17 | Unplug electronics |
| 18 | Use surge protectors and power strips |
| 19 | Use an Energy Hub |
| 20 | Monitor your energy use |
| 21 | Switch to compact fluorescents |
| 22 | Switch to low-flow showerheads |
| 23 | Ask your power company about alternative energy |
| 24 | Get a solar-panel backpack |
| 25 | Telecommute |
| 26 | Bicycle to work |

27   Use public transportation

28   Drive a hybrid

29   Carpool to work

30   Use HOV or carpool lanes

31   Brew your own coffee

32   Use a travel mug

33   Lobby coffee shops for discounts for mug users

34   Know your brew

35   Support Fair Trade coffee

36   Buy shade-grown coffee

37   Brew coffee for carpoolers

38   Bring a travel mug to your carpool-mate

39   Check out Energy Star efficiency ideas

40   Read *50 Simple Things You Can Do to Save the Earth*

41   Turn off the water while brushing your teeth

42   Know your neighbors

43   Smile at your neighbors

44   Keep an eye out for your neighbors and their kids

| 45 | Read *The Death and Life of Great American Cities* |

| 46 | Visit your neighborhood parks |

| 47 | Use your local playgrounds |

| 48 | Support the Play Cities agenda to bring playgrounds to all children |

| 49 | Remind elected officials about the importance of open space |

| 50 | Start a community garden |

| 51 | Create a local play street |

| 52 | Participate in "Won't You Be My Neighbor" Day |

| 53 | Sit on your porch |

| 54 | Say hi to your neighbors |

| 55 | Invite your neighbors into your home |

| 56 | Host neighbors for game nights |

| 57 | Invite neighbors over for TV night |

| 58 | Buy a projector to create big-screen experiences |

| 59 | Make enough food to share |

| 60 | Share an internet connection |

| 61 | Leave your wi-fi network unlocked |

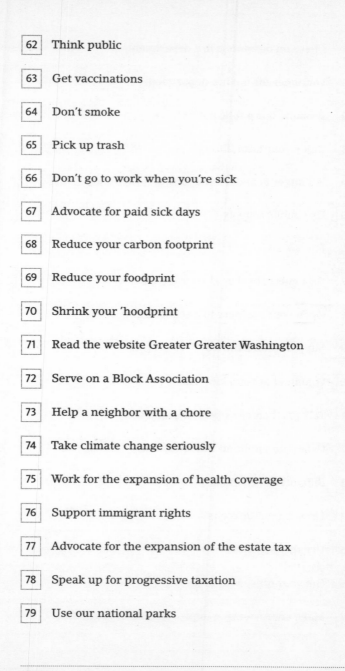

62   Think public

63   Get vaccinations

64   Don't smoke

65   Pick up trash

66   Don't go to work when you're sick

67   Advocate for paid sick days

68   Reduce your carbon footprint

69   Reduce your foodprint

70   Shrink your 'hoodprint

71   Read the website Greater Greater Washington

72   Serve on a Block Association

73   Help a neighbor with a chore

74   Take climate change seriously

75   Work for the expansion of health coverage

76   Support immigrant rights

77   Advocate for the expansion of the estate tax

78   Speak up for progressive taxation

79   Use our national parks

| 80 | Cheer on our public fire department |
| 81 | Volunteer for the fire department |
| 82 | Promote our public police force |
| 83 | Enjoy your local library |
| 84 | Volunteer at and donate to your local library |
| 85 | Use public schools |
| 86 | Join a PTA |
| 87 | Be a guest speaker at your local school |
| 88 | Open your business to a school trip |
| 89 | Support food pantries |
| 90 | Volunteer at soup kitchens |
| 91 | Talk to a homeless person over a meal |
| 92 | Celebrate public access television |
| 93 | Support a seed bank |
| 94 | Drive on public roads |
| 95 | Use the post office |
| 96 | Get your office recycling |
| 97 | Make energy-saving improvements in your office |

| 98 | Switch your workplace to energy-efficient bulbs |
|---|---|
| 99 | Install motion-activated lights at work |
| 100 | Turn off office lights at night |
| 101 | Install low-flush toilets and urinals in your office restrooms |
| 102 | Install hand driers at work restrooms |
| 103 | Install timed faucets at work |
| 104 | Turn off work computers at night |
| 105 | Improve the office kitchen |
| 106 | Stock dishware and utensils in your office kitchen |
| 107 | Have clear cleaning duties in your office kitchen |
| 108 | Provide common condiments and often-used items in your office kitchen |
| 109 | Have a coffeemaker at work |
| 110 | Get rid of the water cooler |
| 111 | Fight the bottled-water business |
| 112 | Relax the office dress code |
| 113 | Relax the office climate control |
| 114 | Create avenues for staff feedback |

| 115 | Provide flex time |
| 116 | Dedicate a staff lounge |
| 117 | Allow independent time at work |
| 118 | Organize staff outings |
| 119 | Build community with your coworkers |
| 120 | Take a green graduation pledge |
| 121 | Advocate for workplace change |
| 122 | Research better business practices |
| 123 | Visit Business.gov for workplace ideas |
| 124 | Anticipate objections to workplace improvements |
| 125 | Invest yourself in workplace improvements |
| 126 | Engage your coworkers about their lives |
| 127 | Make coffee for everyone at work |
| 128 | Start a lunch co-op |
| 129 | Host work socials |
| 130 | Spike the water cooler conversation |
| 131 | Find some common ground |
| 132 | Make sure coworkers are registered to vote |

133 Organize your coworkers

134 Thank labor unions

135 Join Working America

136 Talk with your coworkers about what's important to them

137 Delegate organizing tasks to your coworkers

138 Circulate a petition in your workplace

139 Have a letter-writing campaign at work

140 Identify targets and allies in your workplace

141 "Just do it" to make change at work

142 Say yes to employee ideas to work liberally

143 Understand your business's landscape of workers and community

144 Read *Fast Food Nation*

145 Pay higher than the mimimum wage

146 Offer health benefits

147 Subsidize child care

148 Compensate employees for continuing education

149 Open your business venue for community meetings

150  Donate profits to nonprofits

151  Respect work

152  Listen to your workers

153  Share the wealth

154  Know your community

155  Have a longer—and larger—view

156  Join Net Impact

157  Join the Social Venture Network

158  Shorten, or eliminate, your commute

159  Eliminate office rent and utilities costs

160  Waste less paper

161  Cut down office costs

162  Make your work schedule fit your family schedule

163  Share costly resources with other freelancers

164  Get involved with coworking

165  Join the Freelancers Union

166  Volunteer your professional skills

167  Order beer by the pitcher

168  Read *Bowling Alone*

169  Use Meetup.com

170  Join Green Drinks

171  Join Slow Food USA

172  Love liberally

173  Watch *The Daily Show*

174  Watch the *Colbert Report*

175  Laugh liberally

176  Cheer on Al Franken

177  Watch Mort Sahl routines

178  Check out Lenny Bruce

179  Find old Dick Gregory sets

180  View George Carlin clips

181  Watch Smothers Brothers videos

182  Enjoy Richard Pryor comedy

183  Catch old Ellen DeGeneres material

184  Laugh along with Tina Fey

185  Watch *Guess Who's Coming to Dinner*

186  Rent *Philadelphia*

187  Check out *Superbad*

188  Support Ron Howard films

189  Learn about Participant Films

190  Watch *An Inconvenient Truth*

191  Judge films for their portrayal of women

192  Judge films for their portrayal of people of color

193  Judge films for their portrayal of gay and lesbian characters

194  Judge films for their messages of deference to authority

195  Watch *One Flew Over the Cuckoo's Nest*

196  Ask whether a film trades on love or on violence

197  Check film reviews for liberal themes

198  Look at how movie posters treat women

199  Let your friends see films through your liberal lens

200  Screen liberally

201  Host Brave New Films screenings

202  Support independent movie theaters

203 Research films you want shown

204 Organize friends to request films

205 Approach your local theater to show films

206 Watch *The Grapes of Wrath*

207 Watch *Footloose*

208 For Martin Luther King Jr. Day, watch *4 Little Girls*

209 For Valentine's Day, watch *But I'm a Cheerleader*

210 For Presidents' Day, watch *Dave*

211 For Earth Day, watch *The Age of Stupid*

212 For Memorial Day, watch *The Great Dictator*

213 For the Fourth of July, watch *Good Night, and Good Luck*

214 For Labor Day, watch *Norma Rae*

215 For Halloween, watch *The Last Supper*

216 For Columbus Day, watch *Smoke Signals*

217 For Christmas, watch *It's a Wonderful Life*

218 Play a State of the Union drinking game

219 Host primary night parties

220 Join debate night parties

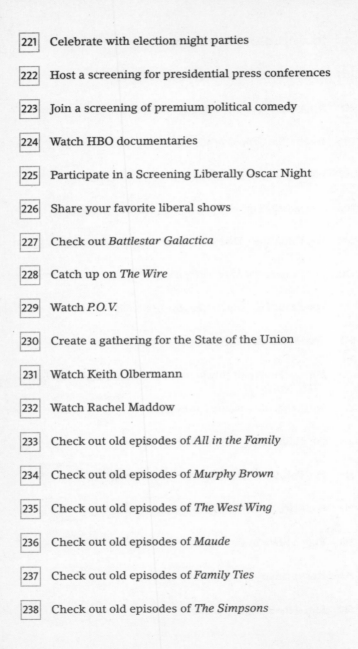

221    Celebrate with election night parties

222    Host a screening for presidential press conferences

223    Join a screening of premium political comedy

224    Watch HBO documentaries

225    Participate in a Screening Liberally Oscar Night

226    Share your favorite liberal shows

227    Check out *Battlestar Galactica*

228    Catch up on *The Wire*

229    Watch *P.O.V.*

230    Create a gathering for the State of the Union

231    Watch Keith Olbermann

232    Watch Rachel Maddow

233    Check out old episodes of *All in the Family*

234    Check out old episodes of *Murphy Brown*

235    Check out old episodes of *The West Wing*

236    Check out old episodes of *Maude*

237    Check out old episodes of *Family Ties*

238    Check out old episodes of *The Simpsons*

239    Check out old episodes of *Saturday Night Live*

240    Check out old episodes of *Sesame Street*

241    Attend a show at The Tank

242    Pay a visit to the Des Moines Social Club

243    Read, see, or stage a production of *Lysistrata*

244    Read, see, or stage a production of *Inherit the Wind*

245    Read, see, or stage a production of *Mother Courage and Her Children*

246    Read, see, or stage a production of *The Cradle Will Rock*

247    Read, see, or stage a production of *Waiting for Lefty*

248    Read, see, or stage a production of *Twelve Angry Men*

249    Read, see, or stage of production of *Master Harold and the Boys*

250    Read, see, or stage a production of *Hair*

251    Read, see, or stage a production of *Les Misérables*

252    Read, see, or stage a production of *Rent*

253    Listen to Public Enemy

254    Listen to Black Star

255    Listen to Le Tigre

256 Listen to Outkast

257 Listen to Radiohead

258 Listen to The Clash

259 Listen to Discount

260 Listen to Marvin Gaye

261 Listen to Fela Kuti

262 Listen to TV on the Radio

263 Listen to Dar Williams

264 Listen to Rage Against the Machine

265 Listen to Bruce Springsteen

266 Listen to Ani DiFranco

267 Take a road trip to historical sites

268 Take a vacation building homes

269 Find tips for environmentally friendly hiking

270 Learn about socially conscious hunting

271 Join Karma Krew

272 Visit minor league ballparks

273 Eat at a local diner

274 Read the local paper

275 Reuse and recycle while traveling

276 Take part in CouchSurfing

277 Tip well

278 Wear sunscreen

279 Join a flash mob

280 Follow Improv Everywhere

281 Carry the spirit of Billionaires for Bush

282 Discredit conservative tropes

283 Honestly assess where we, as a country, fall short

284 Hold up America's liberal themes as an ideal

285 Reread the Declaration of Independence with a liberal lens

286 Reconsider the liberal message of the Revolution of 1800

287 Learn the lessons of abolition

288 Learn the lessons of breaking up the trusts

289 Learn the lessons of women's suffrage

290 Learn the lessons of the New Deal

| 291 | Learn the lessons of our entrance into World War II |
| 292 | Learn the lessons of the Marshall Plan and GI Bill |
| 293 | Learn the lessons of the struggle for civil rights |
| 294 | Reconsider the liberal message of the moon landing |
| 295 | Applaud Thoreau's political protest |
| 296 | Study the achievements of Frances Perkins |
| 297 | Celebrate Repeal of Prohibition |
| 298 | Embrace *Loving vs. Virginia* |
| 299 | Highlight the importance of the resignation of Richard Nixon |
| 300 | Refute that our founders were all slave owners |
| 301 | Reconsider whether the yeoman farmer was the ideal American |
| 302 | Challenge the idea that baseball was born in the countryside |
| 303 | Deny that the 1950s were a time of peace and prosperity |
| 304 | Know that Ronald Reagan did not end the Cold War |
| 305 | Read *1984* |
| 306 | Read *Catch-22* |
| 307 | Read *The Grapes of Wrath* |

308   Read *Slaughterhouse-Five*

309   Read *No Name in the Street*

310   Read *To Kill a Mockingbird*

311   Read *Fahrenheit 451*

312   Read *Beloved*

313   Read *The Shock Doctrine*

314   Read *A People's History of the United States*

315   Read the poetry of Walt Whitman

316   Talk out your thoughts or confusion with others

317   Read more

318   Read magazines

319   Explore a newsstand

320   Check out *Mother Jones*

321   Subscribe to *The Nation*

322   Read *The New Yorker*

323   Pick up some conservative magazines to know their arguments

324   Read *50 Simple Things You Can Do to Fight the Right*

325   Leave a magazine out and open on a library table

326 Organize your library's purchasing power

327 Become your own library

328 Include your name and contact info on books you share

329 Start a reading group

330 Choose something from the library stocks

331 Support liberal publishers

332 Don't make your book club too dry

333 Make everyone in the book club a decider

334 Mix in some living authors with your book selection

335 Read the writings of Frederick Douglass

336 Read the writings of John Steinbeck

337 Read the writings of Elizabeth Cady Stanton

338 Read the writings of Upton Sinclair

339 Host your book club as a potluck

340 Host an author

341 Check out Daily Kos

342 Check out Think Progress

343 Check out Talking Points Memo

344 Check out FireDogLake

345 Check out Jack & Jill Politics

346 Check out Empty Wheel

347 Check out Feministing

348 Check out Open Left

349 Check out FiveThirtyEight

350 Check out Crooks and Liars

351 Check out Eschaton

352 Check out Living Liberally

353 Join the discussion on blogs

354 Share what you learn from blogs

355 Encourage friends to change the channel

356 Ask friends to identify every news channel's bias

357 Give friends a magazine to get them off television

358 Bring politics to the dinner table

359 Question your friends

360 Engage your conservative relatives

361 Talk liberally with non-liberals

362 Create a participatory home

363 Include your children in family decisions

364 Include children in household chores

365 Bring children to your work and your social activities

366 Meet your children's friends and their parents

367 Participate in your kids' activities

368 Be involved in your kids' education

369 Participate in collective childcare

370 Spend one-on-one time with your children

371 Encourage your children to explore

372 Create boundaries and structure for your children

373 Tell stories with your children

374 Share your values with your children

375 Lead by example and demonstrate values to your children

376 Talk to your kids about the environment

377 Explain to your kids the causes you support

378 Discuss the values you see in your children's behavior

379 Be playful

380　Teach inclusion through children's games

381　Encourage games that ask kids to collaborate

382　Play games that inspire creative thinking

383　Start early as you parent liberally

384　Add *The Lorax* to your children's reading list, or read it aloud

385　Add the Harry Potter books to your children's reading list, or read the novels aloud

386　Add *Free to Be You and Me* to your children's reading list, or read it aloud

387　Add Shel Silverstein to your children's reading list, or read his poetry aloud

388　Add Encyclopedia Brown books to your children's reading list, or read them aloud

389　Add *Blubber* to your children's reading list, or read it aloud

390　Add the Lord of the Rings trilogy to your children's reading list, or read the novels aloud

391　Add *The Little Prince* to your children's reading list, or read it aloud

392　Choose a congregation that hosts a CSA

393　Make sure your congregation is taking green steps

| 394 | Ask your congregation to buy food from local vendors |
| 395 | Choose a congregation that uses gender-neutral liturgy |
| 396 | Choose a congregation that accepts female and gay officiants |
| 397 | Choose a congregation that pays workers a living wage |
| 398 | Choose a congregation that organizes service trips |
| 399 | Choose a congregation that has usher-exchange programs with other congregations |
| 400 | Choose a congregation that allows interfaith spouses to participate |
| 401 | Choose a congregation that respects non-congregants |
| 402 | Choose a congregation that respects gender equality |
| 403 | Choose a congregation that respects its gay members |
| 404 | Choose a congregation that invests in community |
| 405 | Choose a congregation that celebrates |
| 406 | Donate to food and clothing drives over the holidays |
| 407 | Give to charity rather than give gifts |
| 408 | Volunteer on holidays |
| 409 | Shop consciously for the holidays |
| 410 | Show goodwill to all |

411 | Shop at mom-and-pop stores

412 | Buy union

413 | Ask where your products are made

414 | Check out the Green Pages

415 | Check out The Responsible Shopper

416 | Learn about the conditions in which workers produce items you buy

417 | Check on the environmental record of a business

418 | Check on the politics of a business

419 | Ask friends for recommendations on conscientious shopping

420 | Offer your own advice on conscientious shopping

421 | Choose items with less packaging

422 | Get a sense of the work environment in the store

423 | Choose items that are biodegradable

424 | Support independent producers and craftspeople

425 | Give feedback to stores

426 | Ask yourself: Do I really need this?

427 | Boycott

| 428 | Buycott |
|-----|---------|
| 429 | Create new markets |
| 430 | Create alternatives |
| 431 | Subscribe to CREDO cell service |
| 432 | Carry a Working Assets credit card |
| 433 | Choose a business that donates profits to good causes |
| 434 | Choose a business that respects its customers |
| 435 | Choose a business that treats workers with respect |
| 436 | Choose a business that embodies ethical practices |
| 437 | Choose a business that markets less |
| 438 | Choose a business that lobbies for the public good |
| 439 | Choose a business that takes action |
| 440 | Patronize the Better World Club |
| 441 | Patronize Organic Valley |
| 442 | Patronize 3R Living |
| 443 | Patronize Etsy |
| 444 | Patronize the Progressive Book Club |
| 445 | Beware: plastic |

| 446 | Buy now: used goods |
| 447 | Beware: made in China |
| 448 | Buy now: local, handmade |
| 449 | Beware: unaccountability |
| 450 | Buy now: anything from a lemonade stand |
| 451 | Eat liberally |
| 452 | Purchase food that is organic |
| 453 | Purchase food that is locally grown |
| 454 | Purchase food that is grass-fed |
| 455 | Purchase food that is Fair Trade |
| 456 | Purchase food that is biodynamic |
| 457 | Consider a retrovore lifestyle |
| 458 | Eat less meat |
| 459 | Cut back on industrially produced eggs and dairy |
| 460 | Support your local food producers |
| 461 | Limit your consumption of processed, convenience foods |
| 462 | Reduce food waste |
| 463 | Convert kitchen scraps into black gold by composting |

464 Take the time to make a meal from scratch

465 Buy food from local shops

466 Shop at farmers' markets

467 Join CSAs/Farm-Shares

468 Join a food co-op

469 Push your supermarkets

470 Advocate for food access

471 Drink locally

472 Support microbrews

473 Try craft beer

474 Toast labor

475 Drink green

476 Drink Magic Hat

477 Drink New Belgium Brewery

478 Drink Maker's Mark

479 Confront the ills of alcohol

480 Drink politically

481 Go dry on Coors

482 Tell Anheuser-Busch to stand against the Chamber

483 Stop drinking Guinness and Johnnie Walker

484 Switch to a credit union

485 Visit the Credit Union Co-op

486 Learn about socially responsible investment

487 Check out the Social Investment Forum

488 Look to Social Funds for ideas on socially responsible investment

489 Learn about Domini for socially responsible investment

490 Start your own investment club

491 Be a conscious shareholder

492 Use those proxy votes

493 Organize a shareholder resolution

494 Sell shares to send a message

495 Ask about distribution of wealth in businesses in which you invest

496 Ask how the business behaves in new communities

497 Ask for a plan to reduce your carbon footprint from businesses in which you invest

498  Get others joining you in asking for better practices
     from businesses in which you invest

499  Elect representatives who reflect our ideals

500  Push those people who are in power

501  Involve ourselves in issues we face as society

502  March in the Fourth of July parade as a liberal

503  Host community barbecues

504  Paint a friend's home with fellow liberals

505  Raise money to pay fines incurred by antiwar activists

506  Do community service along with teens punished for
     antiwar activism

507  Organize safe, legal protests for teens

508  Host a Loving Day celebration

509  Make a social event out of canvassing

510  Host Candidates Gone Wild

511  Host Mayoroke

512  Participate in Trick or Vote

513  Throw a field day party the weekend before Election
     Day

514 Organize blueberry picking to teach agricultural education

515 Take a bike trip to teach open-space advocacy

516 Invite your community to an election day party

517 Support HeadCount

518 Get involved with Get In The Game

519 Make political calls from a park

520 Organize house parties around swing-state calls

521 Throw a party the Sunday before the primary

522 Host a political St. Patrick's Day breakfast

523 Attend the Tom Harkin Steak Fry

524 Contribute to campaigns

525 Work with disenfranchised communities

526 Testify at City Council

527 Make volunteering easy

528 Organize volunteer activities in ways convenient to the volunteers

529 Bring actions to the volunteers

530 Remember to translate for volunteers

| 531 | Make volunteering social |

| 532 | Make it easy to invite friends to volunteer |

| 533 | Keep volunteering casual |

| 534 | Host an after party for volunteers |

| 535 | Make volunteering rewarding |

| 536 | Lay out the big picture to volunteers |

| 537 | Mark progress and celebrate victories with volunteers |

| 538 | Say thank you |